"Having known, loved and walked this journey of ministry with Jack Graham since our teenage years, I can give testimony to the fact that he is a "man of God." These words flow from a pen of integrity and a lifetime of beating out on the anvil of personal experience the godly principles of not only becoming a man of God, but finishing strong."

—Dr. O. S. HAWKINS, CEO/President, GuideStone Financial
Resources

"If I, or anyone else, had any question about how to lead a Christian life, they are answered in Dr. Graham's book. I had sometimes wondered after I received another chance at life what I was to do. Jack Graham's book gave me what I needed to know. *A Man of God* gave me the perfect prescription of how a man should lead a Christian life.

—PAT SUMMERALL, Sports Commentator

"My good friend Jack Graham has a powerful message designed to address a critical need. His message to men is timeless, potent, and biblically sound. It is must reading for any man who desires to be all that God has created him to be and who desires to order his priorities in line with God's. Dr. Graham not only proclaims this message but also has modeled it himself and equipped the men in his church to do the same."

—DR. TONY EVANS, Senior Pastor, Oak Cliff Bible Fellowship,
President, The Urban Alternative

"*A Man of God – Essential Priorities for Every Man's Life* reminds us of how important it is to stop and think about our Christian life. Dr. Graham is straightforward about what's required of disciples, and he clearly outlines the commitments we must make in our daily walk. He eloquently challenges us to continue to grow in our faith and to be passionate in order to impact others."

—ROGER STAUBACH, Hall of Fame Quarterback, Businessman

"Unless you are spiritually and physically fit, you will not know what I call the 'joy of living.' However, I have found that physical fitness is easier to achieve than spiritual fitness. Dr. Graham's book is a "must read" for any man not satisfied with being just a "curious Christian" and who wants to have a committed, "maxed out" relationship with Christ."

—KENNETH H. COOPER, M.D., M.P.H., Author, *Aerobics*

"Jack Graham is a man under authority. He has faithfully served his Master, the Lord Jesus Christ. Jack Graham is a man of integrity. He has lived a life of commitment based upon his faith in the Savior who redeemed him. Jack Graham is a man who loves his family and has provided leadership as a husband and father under the guidance of the Holy Spirit. Jack Graham is a man who answered God's call on his life to preach the whole truth of the gospel. These all embody elements of a new book Jack has written, *A Man of God*. I believe every man who reads through its pages will be challenged to live a life pleasing to Almighty God."

—FRANKLIN GRAHAM, President/CEO,
Billy Graham Evangelistic Association;
President/CEO, Samaritan's Purse

"Jack Graham has a wonderful gift for making the normal Christian life exciting and demanding but fulfilling. In this book he challenges men to understand and then affirm a radical commitment to God. Many men see the Christian faith lacking a masculine component. Dr. Graham challenges men to move beyond the curiosity level to become a fully devoted man for God. This is a call to commitment that requires real men of courage and conviction. Like his powerful, masculine preaching in the pulpit of one of America's greatest churches, Prestonwood Baptist in Dallas, he challenges men to move beyond the flawed "macho" image of masculinity in our culture. A real man has the courage to surrender his will and his future to a loving God with a wonderful plan for his life. Great reading, filled with the stories of men of courage in all walks of life! I would that every man at this university could read this book."
    —DR. DAVID W. CLARK, President, Palm Beach Atlantic University

"Jack Graham knows what it takes to be a strong and sturdy man —partially because he is one himself and partially because he leads so many men through his phenomenal ministry at Prestonwood Baptist Church in Dallas. He writes with a sense of what men want to hear, and this often includes illustrations from athletics, business, and the world of competition. No man reading this book will miss its central point: A great life for a man will involve a deep and disciplined commitment to Christ."
    —DR. NEIL CLARK WARREN, Psychologist, Founder, eHarmony.com

"Every time I hear Jack from the pulpit or read one of his books, I am reminded of how God has gifted him with the ability to communicate in a powerful, straightforward, spirit-filled way; particularly to men. This book will challenge you to deepen your commitment to your personal relationship with Christ. Jack encourages us to be passionate and committed servant-leaders in our families and our churches."
    —RON MURFF, President, Guaranty Bank

"Jack is a man's man and he knows how to get to the bottom line and challenge us to be the men we all desire to be in Christ. This is a must read for real men."
    —DR. TOM MULLINS, Senior Pastor, Christ Fellowship Church

"Jack Graham's latest book has challenged me to the inner depths of my soul. He will challenge you, convict you, and stimulate you in a way that hasn't happened before. Get ready for a life-changing read."
    —PAT WILLIAMS, Senior Vice President, Orlando Magic

"As I read this book, Dr. Graham inspired me and he will inspire you to be maxed our for Jesus Christ. He challenges us to let the Master take charge. Let's go for it!"
    —GARY KINDER, Leader, Bent Tree Bible Study, Businessman

# A
# MAN
# OF
# GOD

*Essential Priorities for*
*Every Man's Life*

## STUDY GUIDE EDITION

## JACK GRAHAM

### FOREWORD BY CHUCK NORRIS

**:: CROSSWAY**
WHEATON, ILLINOIS

*A Man of God: Essential Priorities for Every Man's Life*
*(Study Guide Edition)*

Copyright © 2005, 2007 by Jack Graham

Published by Crossway
        1300 Crescent Street
        Wheaton, Illinois 60187

First edition 2005

Study Guide edition 2007

Cover design: Josh Dennis

First printing 2005

Printed in the United States of America

The study guide was produced with the assistance of The Livingstone Corporation (www.LivingStoneCorp.com). Project staff includes Dave Veerman and Neil Wilson.

Unless otherwise marked, Scripture references are from the *New King James Version*. Copyright © 1982, Thomas Nelson, Inc. Used by permission.

Scripture references marked NIV are from *The Holy Bible: New International Version.*® Copyright © 1973, 1978, 1984 by International Bible Society. Used by permission of Zondervan Publishing House. All rights reserved.

The "NIV" and "New International Version" trademarks are registered in the United States Patent and Trademark Office by International Bible Society. Use of either trademark requires the permission of International Bible Society.

"Rise up, O Men of God!" words by William P. Merrill (Richmond, Va.: *The Presbyterian Outlook*).

ISBN 13: 978-1-58134-874-3
ISBN 10: 1-58134-874-6

**Library of Congress Cataloging-in-Publication Data**
Graham, Jack, 1950-
  A man of God : essential priorities for every man's life / Jack Graham.
 — Study guide ed.
    p. cm.
  Includes indexes.
  ISBN 13: 978-1-58134-874-3 (tpb)
  1. Christian men—Religious life. I. Title.
BV4528.2.G72      2007
248.8'42—dc22                  2006032421

Crossway is a publishing ministry of Good News Publishers.

VP      21   20   19   18   17   16   15   14
16   15   14   13   12   11   10   9   8   7   6

*I dedicate this book to my grandfather,*

A. J. SIMS.

*He read me the Scriptures, led me to childlike faith in Christ,*
*and demonstrated the life of a godly man.*
*Though he has been in heaven many years,*
*the legacy of his life lives on.*
*I am forever grateful.*

# CONTENTS

# FOREWORD

*By Chuck Norris*

MY GOOD FRIEND AND PASTOR, Dr. Jack Graham, has an incredible way—a gift, really—of communicating. Go to Prestonwood Baptist Church on any given weekend, or listen to him daily on PowerPoint, and you'll find yourself engrossed in his sermons. His messages are scriptural, yet cultural. He reaches deep within the Word and eloquently communicates it to thousands in an easy-to-understand manner.

As gifted as he is in communicating to the body of Christ as a whole, Dr. Graham's gift is multiplied as a teacher of men. We hear it said often of actors or athletes that a particular man is a "man's man." Well, Jack Graham is not only a man's man; he's a man of God who speaks so effectively to the hearts of men.

I started attending Prestonwood a few years back, and his sermons kept me riveted. I returned every time I was in town. His messages helped me to see things more clearly in my life, helped me to keep the main thing, the main thing.

As men, we struggle with many things in life. How can we not, when society's Mount Everest expectations of us are so completely unreachable we kill ourselves just trying to reach Base Camp, much less the summit? We're not quite brawny or brainy enough. Our careers are at a standstill. Our marriages sometimes seem like they're in reverse rather than drive. Our children are headed down the wrong paths, and we can't seem to ever say the right thing. Our finances are in shambles, yet we're still trying to keep up with the next guy.

"Is this all there is?" we ask ourselves. Absolutely not. And that's why it's a great privilege to recommend to you *A Man of God*.

Dr. Graham tells us we're "maxed out" on all the wrong things. It's the Lord for whom we need to give our all. It is He for whom we should lead our lives. "The Christian life is more important than the Super Bowl, the World Series, the NBA Finals, and the Stanley Cup all wrapped up together," Dr. Graham writes. And he's right, because, really, in the end what else matters?

My pastor's teachings, like this volume you're holding, are a blessing in my life. This book will help each of you in your journey to become the man you truly want to be: a better husband and father, a man pure of heart and pure of mind, a disciple and mentor—a man of God.

# INTRODUCTION

THROUGH THE YEARS I have firmly believed that if revival is to come to the church, and if the Good News of Jesus Christ is to spread to the nations, it will be because men became godly and began living their faith with passion and integrity.

I am fully aware that committed women have often taken up the spiritual responsibilities of families, churches, and communities. Without question, godly women have assumed a strategic role in world evangelism and have led the way in shaping our families and the future.

Having said that, I firmly believe it is time for men to step up to the challenges of the twenty-first century. We are facing profound moral, ethical, domestic, and international issues that mark a culture in need of answers. What we need are spiritual men who will shape the future and change the world. But frankly, many men are not responding to the call, even though their influence is needed more today than at any other time in history. Now is the time for men to keep their promises and live their principles.

My prayer is that this book will be a stimulus in raising up a generation of men who will say, "For the sake of the Kingdom, for the sake of my family, for the sake of God's church, and for the sake of our nation, I will become a man of God."

This book describes what this kind of man is like and how he lives his life. My prayer is that some thought, illustration, or biblical principle will move you from being just a man to being a man of God!

Men, it's time to get real and to get radical for Jesus. Remember this: "The eyes of the LORD run to and fro throughout the whole earth, to show Himself strong on behalf of those whose heart is loyal to Him" (2 Chronicles 16:9).

In this critical hour of history, may our great God find us faithful and loyal and strengthen us to the task at hand. Join me in praying, "Lord, may I be a godly man and may I be used for Your glory until You come."

Rise up, O men of God!
Have done with lesser things.
Give heart and mind and soul and strength
To serve the King of kings.

# Acknowledgments

EVERY BOOK IS A PROJECT and process that involves many dedicated people. I am very grateful for the team that enabled me to offer this book:

To the men of Prestonwood Baptist Church, whose commitment to Christ stirs their pastor's heart. This book is a testimony to your devotion.

To the staff of Prestonwood, men and women who inspire me and motivate me to be a man of God.

To Geri Brady, who assists me in our daily ministry and enables me to get the job done, including this book.

To Philip Rawley, my editor and friend, who understands the call and helps me to deliver the Word with clarity.

To Marvin Padgett and my friends at Crossway Books, I am grateful for the integrity of your work and the opportunity of publishing with you.

To my wife, Deb, our sons Jason and Josh, our daughter Kelly, our daughter-in-law Toby, and our grandson, Ian. You are the biggest reason I want to be a man of God.

PART ONE

# A MAN OF GOD
# AND
# HIS MASTER

# 1

# A Commitment to Maximum Discipleship

I HAD AN INCREDIBLE opportunity to witness a piece of baseball history being made during the 2003 World Series between the New York Yankees and the Florida Marlins.

Along with about 65,000 other people, I was at Pro Player Park in Miami the night that Yankees pitcher Roger Clemens started what was thought at the time to be the final game of his illustrious twenty-one-year career. Thanks to the kindness of friends, I was sitting in the first row behind home plate as Clemens took the mound and proceeded to pitch his heart out.

Clemens had a rough first inning, but then he settled down and began to pitch with the competitive fire that has always been his trademark. I sat there watching this forty-one-year-old man throwing fastballs up to ninety-six miles an hour, putting down the Marlins inning after inning. Clemens pitched through the seventh inning, and by then even the Marlins fans were screaming for him. His last pitch was a ninety-six-mile-per-hour fastball that struck out the batter.

As Clemens walked off the mound, the fans rose in a thunderous wave of cheers—and then, something remarkable began to happen. The Marlins players tipped their hats to him, both those on the field and those standing in the dugout. The Marlins manager also tipped his hat to Clemens and did a slight bow, as if to say, "You were one of the best." It was an electrifying experience to see and hear this tribute to a man who had dedicated himself to his craft and had given everything he had to the game. It was one of the greatest moments I have ever experienced in sports.

What I saw that night at the World Series was a man who "maxed out" in his career. And the fact that Roger Clemens later changed his mind about retirement and returned to baseball in 2004 did nothing to dim the impact of that incredible October evening in Florida. Clemens gave baseball the very best he had, right down to his last pitch, holding nothing back. And when he left the field that night, there was no doubt in anyone's mind about what Roger Clemens had accomplished.

My brother, that's the way I want to live my Christian life! I want to "max out" for the Lord, because the Christian life is more important than the Super Bowl, the World Series, the NBA Finals, and the Stanley Cup all wrapped up together. If the Christian life is worth living, then it's worth the best we can give in terms of our commitment, abilities, and gifts. I want to make sure that I give Jesus Christ everything I have to give, and leave nothing undone that He wanted me to accomplish.

We stood and honored Roger Clemens that night in Florida, and that was fine. But I am praying for myself and all of us as Christian men that when we leave the field of this life, we will leave as men whom our wives, children, coworkers, and friends can honor because we gave our best for Jesus Christ. And most of all, I want to hear Jesus say when I stand before Him, "Well done, good and faithful servant" (Matthew 25:21).

I believe that you and many other Christian men want this too, which is why I wrote this book to help you in that quest. You see, I believe that it is not only possible for you and me to be men of honor in God's eyes and the eyes of others, I believe this is what He expects of us as men who have put our faith in Jesus Christ.

## YOU CAN BE THE KIND OF MAN GOD IS SEEKING

There's a lot of talk today about what it takes to be a man. Gender roles in our culture are probably more confused today than they have ever been, and in this environment it's sometimes hard to know what being a man is all about.

One idea of manhood that has been popular for a long time is the macho man, epitomized for many of us by the Marlboro man in the old cigarette ads. This guy was a rugged cowboy who was clearly his own man—tough, confident, always in control, able to outride, outshoot, outrope, and outfight any guy around. His vocabulary was basically "Yup" and "Nope." Anything more than that was a lot of useless chatter.

But the sixties brought us a new image of manhood that was mellow instead of macho—the "sensitive man." This is the guy who is "in touch with his feelings." All of a sudden people started talking about a man's feminine side and how men didn't need to be afraid to let this side of their personality come through. One radio station in Dallas poked fun at this concept with a fictional "Sensitive Male Hotline" that men could call to discuss these issues and express their feelings.

These two images of manhood are still around. But for Christian men the issue is not whether we should be macho or mellow. We need to be maxed-out men for Jesus Christ, wholly sold out to Him and giving Him the best we have.

Now I didn't say we need to burn ourselves out. There's a big difference between burning out and maxing out. God didn't call any man to drive himself so hard that he flames out and wastes away. I'm talking about maximizing your strengths, your commitment, and your devotion to the Lord Jesus Christ.

We get a glimpse into the kind of men God is looking for in 2 Chronicles 16:9: "For the eyes of the LORD run to and fro throughout the whole earth, to show Himself strong on behalf of those whose heart is loyal to Him." God is looking for men who will steadfastly give their whole hearts to Him. Paul was that kind of man. "For to me, to live is Christ, and to die is gain," he declared (Philippians 1:21). Jesus called us to this same high standard when He said, "Seek first the kingdom of God and His righteousness, and all these things shall be added to you" (Matthew 6:33).

If we're going to be successful in our Christian lives, it means putting Christ first and living radically for Him.

Now I know that the idea of being a radical isn't popular in our post-9/11 culture where religious radicals are the bad guys. Most of us don't want to be labeled as a "Jesus freak" or an extremist on religion. So we often settle for something less than maxing out for Christ.

But the fact is that radical Christian living, maximum commitment to the Lord, is really the normal Christian life. Anything else is abnormal. The late Vance Havner used to say that most Christians are living so abnormally—so far below what God wants—that if they lived normally, it would seem abnormal.

Do you hear what that great old preacher was saying? God is not just looking for a few "super saints" who will rise above the norm and do great things for Him. He wants those who are willing to say, "My heart is steadfast and loyal and committed to You." That's something all of us can do, regardless of our abilities or gifts.

So let me ask you: Do words like powerful, passionate, successful, and joyful describe your Christian life? Are you living with purpose? Your purpose is the reason God put you here on earth. It's essential to discover your purpose, but you also need passion because it is the fire that feeds your purpose. Once you know the God-given purpose for your life and are fired with a holy passion to accomplish it, there isn't anything the devil can throw at you that will stop you.

## MAXIMUM COMMITMENT
## MEANS BECOMING JESUS' DISCIPLE

Maximum commitment is actually a very simple thing. It means to become a disciple of Jesus Christ. You can see the root of the word *discipline* in this concept of being a disciple. Discipleship is placing ourselves under the discipline and training of Christ, submitting ourselves to the authority of God's Word, and then living in daily devotion to what we are learning. A disciple is basically a learner, a student. Jesus said, "It is enough for a disciple that he be like his teacher" (Matthew 10:25). Christian discipleship is learning and practicing the discipline of Jesus so that we become like Him.

## Take Your Life Off "Cruise Control"

Don't you love all the gadgets and luxuries they have on cars these days? I learned that cruise control has actually been around since 1945, although most of us probably didn't have it on our first cars. But now we can cruise for hours and just enjoy the drive.

Putting cruise control on a car was a great idea. But I'm afraid that too many Christian men have put their spiritual lives on cruise. They're just rolling along. The problem with this is that when we are running on automatic pilot instead of being committed to the Lord's call to be His disciples, we may get too comfortable cruising to stop and turn around when we start going the wrong way.

Men are good at that. Our wives look at the map and say, "I think we're lost," and we come back with, "Nah, that's impossible. I know exactly where we are. Besides, we're making such good time, I don't want to stop." But the truth is that we are as lost as a ball in tall weeds. We are just too embarrassed or too prideful to stop and ask for directions.

I'm not talking about being lost in terms of our salvation; I mean wandering all over creation rather than getting to God's desired destination, and doing it effectively. There is nothing automatic about Christian discipleship, especially if we intend to practice maximum commitment to Christ.

We must make a daily decision to pick up our cross, deny ourselves, and follow Christ (see Mark 8:34). No one said it was going to be easy. Jesus demands every ounce of devotion from His disciples. Nothing—not business nor even family—is to stand in the way of our all-out commitment to Him.

## Don't Expect to "Microwave" Spiritual Maturity

For some men a microwave oven is a necessity, not a luxury. One thing we love about microwaves is that they only take about two to three minutes to get the job done.

Now be honest. Do you stand in front of the microwave while you're heating something up and say, "Come on, come on, come on!"? Maybe you keep looking in the little window, or pace back and forth waiting for the timer to go off. And we also get edgy waiting for our computers to boot up in the morning.

It's amazing, isn't it? We live in a world in which we expect to get whatever we want *now*. Our culture feeds the impatience that seems to be built into men when it comes to many of the routines of life. The trouble is we can carry this microwave mentality over into our Christian lives, which is as futile as trying to run your spiritual life on cruise control.

I hope you have discovered that there is no such thing as instant discipline or maturity in the Christian life. You can't say to God, "Okay, I'm ready to walk with You. Just email or fax me the stuff I need so I can get it done this week. I want to be a spiritual man, but I don't have a lot of time."

The fact is that you can't hurry holiness or speed up the work of God in your life. You must be willing to take time and pay the price necessary to train yourself in godly living.

## Change Your Mind About the Christian Life

As we gear up for this study, I'm asking you to consider a new way of thinking about the Christian life. We need to let go of the idea that we can be a Christian without getting in too deep or messing up our comfort; that we can read our Bible when we feel like it or pray only when we're in a crisis; that we can go to church and worship God when it's convenient; or that we can witness to others as long as it doesn't embarrass us. I want us as Christian men to put away these ideas and take God's call to commitment seriously.

One day Jesus said to a tax collector named Levi, who was also known as Matthew, "Follow Me" (Luke 5:27). That sounds simple enough, but notice Matthew's response: "So he left all, rose up, and followed Him" (v. 28). Matthew quit his lucrative job to follow Jesus. Peter, Andrew, John, and James did the same thing (see Matthew 4:18-22).

In other words, following Jesus is a call to maximum commitment. It means walking in the same direction and the same way that He walked, and it means doing it every day. That's clear from the form of the command Jesus used when He said to Matthew, "Follow Me." This is a verb form that implies continuous action. We could render it, "Follow Me and keep on following Me." To follow Jesus means to share His life and be His companion.

At this point you may be wondering what your life will start looking like when you follow Jesus in all-out, maximum commitment. Several wonderful things will happen.

### YOU WILL PUT JESUS FIRST IN YOUR LIFE

When you truly decide to follow Jesus' call to discipleship, you will begin to put Him first in your life and give Him your best, not just what's left over after everyone else has gotten a piece of you.

I'm not just talking about money, although that certainly is involved in putting Christ first and going all out for Him. But too often we also give Him the leftovers of our time, our energies, our schedule, and other areas that reveal where our priorities truly lie. If you think following Christ sounds costly, you're right. But anything less is hedging on your commitment.

I heard a good illustration of this in a story about a farmer who had two brand new calves. He was a Christian, so he prayed, "Lord, I'm going to give You one of my calves. I'll sell it and use all the money for Your work."

The farmer was so proud of himself for this sacrifice that he told his wife, "Honey, I just promised the Lord that I'm going to give Him one of my new calves." His wife told him how wonderful he was for making such a promise.

But a short time later, the farmer came in for dinner one night looking very despondent. When his wife asked him what was wrong, he looked at her and said sadly, "Honey, the Lord's calf just died."

That's how many Christians treat God. But He won't settle for anything less than wholehearted commitment. It's a matter of priorities, which is an area we struggle in as men. But one way we discover our purpose in life is by getting our priorities straight.

It's ironic that even though we have this ongoing struggle to keep our own priorities and commitments in line, most of us don't respect men who are wishy-washy and can't keep a commitment. I have a friend who bought a new house and then spent months trying to get the painter to come back and redo some work he messed up. A routine developed every week in which my friend would call the painter, who would guarantee to be there the next morning and would ask what time was best and if someone would be home. He even stopped by the house one morning and personally assured my friend's wife that he would come back first thing the next morning. But the guy never showed up, and he eventually quit answering my friend's calls.

That painter would have been a lot more honest if he had said right up front, "Look, I don't like messing around with touch-ups and I have no intention of doing your work. So you might as well quit bugging me." That wouldn't have been good news to my friend, but at least he would have known where he stood and would have saved himself months of frustration and waiting.

This story reminds me of a church in the New Testament that had a problem taking a stand. The risen Jesus Christ had nothing good to say about the church at Laodicea, because it made Him sick.

What was it about this church that nauseated the Lord? He told them, "I know your works, that you are neither cold nor hot. I could wish you were cold or hot. So then, because you are lukewarm, and neither cold nor hot, I will vomit you out of My mouth" (Revelation 3:15-16).

Now I like cold milk and I like hot milk, especially when you put some Hershey's cocoa in it. But have you ever tasted lukewarm milk? Terrible. It's not cold enough to taste good, and it's not hot enough to dissolve the cocoa. About all you can do with lukewarm milk is toss it down the drain.

Jesus is saying to us, "I would rather you be all out, full throttle for Me, or all out against Me! But don't try to straddle the fence and give Me half-hearted devotion."

A lot of people in the church would read those verses and say, "Well, Lord, at least give me *some* credit for being lukewarm. I know I'm not where I ought to be, but give me a break. At least I'm getting warm."

But Jesus said, "No, you have to choose. Either follow Me in total commitment or quit playing the game."

Now don't misunderstand. Jesus wasn't talking about people who are walking with Him in discipleship and seeking to grow, but who make mistakes and slip along the way. Even the apostle Paul, the greatest Christian who ever lived, said, "I haven't arrived yet; I'm still pressing on toward the prize" (see Philippians 3:13-14). Jesus was talking about people who have worn out a church pew for years and yet are no more mature spiritually today than they were ten or twenty years ago.

These are strong words in Revelation 3:15-16, and if left to ourselves we probably would not hold each other to such a high standard. But I have to say that as a pastor, I understand why this is so important. I've seen people file in and out of church for many years without leaving any mark other than a dent in the pew. Every pastor has to deal with the fallout from people who try to give God half-hearted, lukewarm commitment. Jesus calls us to so much more, and it starts with putting Him first in everything.

### YOU WILL BEGIN TO PRODUCE SPIRITUAL FRUIT

Another result you will see when you decide to "max out" for Christ is that you will begin to produce spiritual fruit. John 15:1-17 is a classic passage on spiritual fruit-bearing. As Jesus gathered His men around Him in the Upper Room just before He went to the cross, He wanted to tell them how they were going to carry on His work after He was gone. He promised to send the Holy Spirit to indwell them (John 14:26), and then in chapter 15 He revealed the importance of abiding in Him. Jesus declared that He is the vine, and His disciples are the branches (vv. 1, 5). Because of that relationship, the key to bearing spiritual fruit is, "Abide in Me, and I in you. As the branch cannot bear fruit of itself, unless it abides in the vine, neither can you, unless you abide in Me" (v. 4).

The exciting thing about abiding in Christ, which simply means to remain or continue in Him, is that we become more productive as we grow and draw our strength from Him. Look at the progression in John 15: from "fruit" to "more fruit" to "much fruit" (vv. 2, 8). You don't have to grunt and groan and pour sweat to produce spiritual fruit. All you have to do is "abide" in Jesus the Vine. Fruit is actually a by-product of putting Him first in your life.

Paul described this fruit as "the fruit of the Spirit" that consists of "love, joy, peace, longsuffering, kindness, goodness, faithfulness, gentleness, self-control" (Galatians 5:22-23). Spiritual fruit is the character of Christ produced in our hearts by the power of the Holy Spirit, which gives evidence that we truly belong to Him.

In John 15:16 we learn that this is fruit that will "remain." The fruit we bear for Christ in terms of our love, devotion, and service to Him, and people we win for Him, will last for eternity. Even a cup of water that we give to someone in Jesus' name will be rewarded (Mark 9:41).

### You Will Enjoy the Intimacy of Christ's Presence

There are few images in Scripture that portray a more vital and intimate relationship with Christ than this truth that He wants us to abide in Him. It speaks of constant communion and connection, of living in and enjoying the Lord's presence the way you would do with the person you love the most on earth. This enjoyment comes not only from the fact that you are in a love relationship with a living Person, but also because you sense His smile of approval as you embrace His will and fulfill His purpose for you.

The response that abiding in Christ calls for on our part is wholehearted obedience. I love the definition of the Christian life which calls it "a long obedience in the same direction." I'm more concerned with the *direction* than the *perfection* of your life. None of us will ever achieve perfection, but too many believers become distracted, discouraged, and defeated as the world's pleasures and cares draw them off into side streets that lead to dead ends.

When we are not abiding in Christ—not spending time with Him in the secret place, opening His Word and seeking Him in prayer—we are moving in the wrong direction and need to turn around. Now please know that I am not talking about "toughing out" the Christian life by gritting our teeth and hanging on. Men like to take the approach that says, "I'm going to grind out this Christian life even if it kills me." Well, let me assure you that if you try to live for Christ in your own power, it *will* kill you! It will kill your intimacy and joy, just as it would in your marriage if you told your wife, "I'm going to grind out this marriage even if it kills me."

Intimacy is one of those things that can be incredibly strong, yet also easily broken. It requires a daily decision to keep falling in love with Jesus and to seek Him first in prayer, in worship, and in obedience.

## DECIDE TODAY TO GO ALL OUT FOR CHRIST

Have you noticed how quickly we can lose it in terms of our daily relationship with Christ? I don't mean that we fall into gross sin, but we just stop doing the things that keep us close to Him. It's very much like a marriage in which one or both parties quit taking the time to talk and to do the little acts of kindness and service that say, "I love you. You're on my heart every day. I can't wait to spend time with you."

The importance of our daily walk with Christ can also be illustrated by the discipline of exercise. You can be in really good condition, running or working out regularly and feeling good. But what happens when you lay off the routine for a week or a month or two—or in some cases, for a decade or two? Try to get back in the groove, and your body will quickly let you know that the two of you have been seriously out of touch!

The problem we often encounter when we try to exercise is

that our aging bodies work against us and impede our progress. The same is true in the spiritual life. We have a new nature and the indwelling Holy Spirit as believers in Jesus Christ, but we still have the residue of our old nature, which the Bible calls the flesh.

Paul said, "The flesh lusts against the Spirit, and the Spirit against the flesh; and these are contrary to one another, so that you do not do the things that you wish" (Galatians 5:17). We've all felt this conflict, and God has provided for victory over the flesh. But if we begin neglecting our daily fellowship with Christ, we'll inevitably start fulfilling the lusts of the flesh rather than walking in the Spirit.

There's a famous painting called *Light of the World* that hangs in St. Paul's Cathedral in London. It pictures Jesus standing at the door of a cottage, holding a lantern and knocking. Artist William Holman Hunt's inspiration for this work was Revelation 3:20: "Behold, I stand at the door and knock. If anyone hears My voice and opens the door, I will come in to him and dine with him, and he with Me."

Many homes used to have a print of this painting on their walls because it was so well known. The cottage is one of those old English cottages, and it looks neglected, with thistles and vines overgrowing it. Hunt painted it to represent a neglected, wasted Christian life in which Christ is on the outside seeking intimate fellowship with the person inside. It's quite a contrast: Jesus, the King of the universe, knocking at the door of this humble little house, patiently awaiting admittance into the life of His own child.

When the painting was first displayed, someone asked Hunt if he had made a mistake. "There's no latch on the outside of the door. Jesus couldn't get in if He wanted to."

Hunt simply smiled and said, "That's no mistake. The latch is only on the inside because the person inside has to open it." He's right, because that's exactly what Jesus said. "If anyone hears My voice and opens the door, I will come in." Jesus is not going to beat the door down and burst into your life. He waits for you to open the door.

You may have noticed that Revelation 3:20 was spoken to the church at Laodicea, which we read about earlier. This is a picture of Jesus standing outside the door of His own church and the hearts of His own people, seeking entrance for intimate fellowship and communion. Instead of leaving our Lord on the outside, let's invite Him to be at home in our hearts.

When you do that, your life is going to burst with new light and a new dynamic as a believer with maximum commitment. This is the kind of men needed today—men who follow Jesus with their whole hearts in a half-hearted world and even a half-hearted church.

# 2

# What It Means to Follow the Master

You may remember the name Michael DeBakey. He is one of the world's foremost heart surgeons, a pioneer in areas such as heart bypass operations and heart transplants. His dedication to his field is evident from his encyclopedic list of awards, honors, and writings in addition to the more than 60,000 cardiovascular procedures he has performed.

Dr. DeBakey has also trained many heart surgeons in his long career. He is reported to have told one group of medical students, "I can teach you to be great heart surgeons, but it will demand your total dedication and cost you your time, your marriages, your families—everything you have."

We are shocked when we hear something like this, because it sounds so radical and costly. Whatever we may think of Dr. DeBakey's blunt statement, at least none of his students could come back later and say, "I want out of this deal. I had no idea it was going to cost me everything to follow you. You weren't honest about what it would take to be your disciple in heart surgery."

When I think about this story, it makes me wonder sometimes if the church has always been straightforward with Christians about what it costs to be Jesus' disciple. There is a price to be paid if you and I want to be fully devoted followers of Christ. I want to talk about that price, but also about the wonderful rewards that come when we abandon ourselves to the Lordship of Jesus Christ.

Now when you read the words "fully devoted follower of Christ," your reaction may be, "Wait a minute, Jack. I want to live for Christ, but I haven't arrived yet. I'm making progress, but I've got a long way to go."

That's okay, brother, because none of us has arrived. Remember, the issue is not your perfection, but your direction. Are you moving toward Christian maturity, or away from it? Maybe a better question would be, Are you a fully *developing* follower of Jesus Christ? We may not be perfectly devoted, but we can be developing—growing in the love and grace of Jesus Christ. Is the desire of your heart that Jesus be the Master of your life? That's the kind of commitment He is looking for in men who would be His disciples.

## IT TAKES A PASSION FOR CHRIST TO BE HIS DISCIPLE

Many times when we hear the word *disciple,* we equate it with being a Christian. The two terms are often used interchangeably, yet Jesus Himself seemed to distinguish between salvation and discipleship in Luke 14, a portion of which we are going to consider in detail below.

In Luke 14:16-24, Jesus told a parable that offered a wide-open, all-inclusive invitation to salvation. Any and everyone who would come was welcome to the banquet, which is a picture of salvation. No distinction was made among the invited people, and no requirements were made of them except to come and partake of the banquet.

But then in Luke 14:25-35, Jesus turned to focus more sharply on the cost of following Him as His disciples. The all-out commitment He called for on the part of His followers was a commitment to follow Him in sold-out discipleship, not just salvation.

Jesus' teaching in Luke 14 suggests that it is possible for a person to receive Him as Savior, to begin to follow Him, and yet not bear fruit or be faithful in the Christian life. Both the Bible's teaching and my experience as a pastor tell me that we can believe and belong to the family of God, and yet not commit ourselves in true discipleship and complete devotion to Christ.

### We Need a Passion to Grow to Be Jesus' Disciple

The word *disciple* itself speaks of this deep commitment. It literally means a "learner," or pupil. The idea is that the pupil studies, learns, and grows until he knows what his master wants him to know and is able to do what his master wants him to do. Jesus gave us a classic statement of this when He said, "It is enough for a disciple that he be like his teacher" (Matthew 10:25). It seems clear that Jesus did not just want people to give Him their hearts in salvation, but also to give Him their lives in sold-out discipleship. Whether to answer that call to discipleship is a decision each believer has to make.

A lot of guys think that being a disciple is the top rung on the Christian ladder, so to speak, the highest level of commitment, that only the few and the strong ever reach. But that's not the case. Being a fully developing and growing disciple of Jesus Christ is within the reach of every man, and it is God's will for every believer. It's true that not every born-again Christian is a disciple in the sense I am describing, but that's not because God only chooses a select few. Any man who wants to be Jesus' disciple is welcome to take up his cross and follow Him. But it's definitely a commitment of your life. Just as you cannot be "sort of" married, you can't be a "sort of" disciple of Jesus Christ. It's an exclusive commitment.

That's why, whenever I speak to men, I talk about paying the price and staying the course to be Jesus' disciples. It's time for us as men to get real about our faith. God isn't looking for perfect men, but He is seeking real men—husbands and fathers and workers on the job who are sold out to Christ and who demonstrate the reality of their devotion in every area of their lives.

People respect a man of fierce commitment and passion, even if they disagree with the thing he is passionate about. That's why I am concerned about the *laissez-faire,* anemic kind of Christianity that's being lived by so many men today. It won't pass muster with Jesus, and it won't make anyone else hungry to have what we have.

Someone has said that unbelievers may be lost, but they're not stupid. Most men don't have any desire to buy into a program that seems to produce nothing but half-hearted, weak-kneed followers who don't make any impact.

When Bill Gates was building Microsoft, he wanted to recruit a key man who was moving up the ladder at the giant Pepsico corporation. Gates challenged the man to leave his company and join him in revolutionizing the world of communication by asking him, "Do you want to sell sugared water, or do you want to help change the world?" The man couldn't resist a challenge like that and came on board at Microsoft.

## We Need a Passion for Impact to Be Jesus' Disciple

God has called us as His followers to change the world, not just to sit behind a desk or take up space. You don't have to be a corporate executive to make a difference, because the exciting truth is that any man who is willing to follow Jesus with his whole heart can be a disciple who makes a telling impact for Him.

I think we often do people a disservice when they come forward in church to accept Christ. We tell them to sit down on the front row—and a lot of Christians have been sitting there ever since! But the Christian life is a matter of becoming a world changer, a difference maker, and I have an exhilarating sense that many Christian men are tired of settling for less than the best in their spiritual lives.

We hear a lot about the dumbing down of America, especially in public education. This refers to the constant lowering of standards so that every student can make the grade and advance to the next level, regardless of whether they are learning anything. This is done largely because our culture is deathly afraid that if we set the standard too high, some students may not make it and then they will feel bad about themselves.

This dumbing-down effect is lethal to young people because,

even though they may be handed their diplomas and sent out into the world, they haven't learned what they needed to learn. They haven't been properly *discipled,* in other words. The result is that their growth is stunted and their lives are often unproductive.

Spiritual dumbing down is lethal too. As men of God, we can't buy into people or programs that "dumb down" the Christian life to make it more acceptable and seem less demanding. It's time for us to raise the bar, not lower it so that being a disciple of Christ means little more than showing up on Sunday and doing the best we can the rest of the week. It's time for Christian men to lift up the standard of Jesus Christ rather than living for lesser things.

We are called to commitment, so if words like "exciting," "challenging," and "dynamic" do not describe your walk with Christ, then it's time to take a new look at the way you are walking and where you are going. If you want to be the kind of disciple I've been describing, you may need to change your way of thinking about your relationship with Christ.

We all need to check the vitality of our Christian lives regularly. That's why I want to take you to Luke 14:25-33, where Jesus confronted a large crowd of followers and would-be disciples by spelling out what it really cost to be His disciple.

## THERE ARE DEMANDS WE HAVE TO MEET TO BE JESUS' DISCIPLE

Before we look at this text we need to understand what was happening at this stage in Jesus' earthly ministry. The Lord was incredibly popular at this particular moment. The crowds that followed Him were large and enthusiastic. Jesus spoke like no man had ever spoken, and the people hung on His words. It seemed that almost everyone in Israel wanted to be Jesus' disciple.

But Jesus knew that His popularity with the masses was based largely on the magnificent miracles He performed and the fact that He could feed a crowd with a little boy's lunch. The people figured that anyone who could heal all their diseases and feed them was someone they wanted to be around. Since Jesus "knew what was in man" (John 2:25), He knew the majority of these followers weren't interested in being His disciples. They simply admired Him.

Actually, that crowd's reaction to Jesus is still common today. Jesus has been admired throughout history as a great teacher and leader. H. G. Wells, the noted historian who was not a believer in Christ, nevertheless put Jesus at the top of his list of the ten greatest men in human history.

Every Sunday our Dallas newspaper features a profile of a prominent local person. This person is given a list of questions to answer, including the people he or she would invite to their fantasy dinner. Many people over the years have said they would invite Jesus Christ, among other famous people from history, although it's safe to say that not all of those interviewed have been born-again believers.

The crowds of Jesus' day simply followed the excitement and climbed onto the bandwagon while Jesus was popular because it was the religious thing to do. Those kinds of folks are still around today.

Our churches are crowded with people who claim to know Jesus. But there is nothing in their lives to give any indication that they have a saving relationship with Christ. The truth is they are lost churchgoers. They like going to church because the crowd is there and everybody else is doing it, so why not? Others may come because it's good for their business or social connections to be seen in church. But whatever their reason for coming, multitudes of people are following Jesus the way the crowd in Luke 14 followed Him. They're just going along with everyone else to bask in the excitement.

## We Must Love Jesus More
## Than Any Human Relationship

Jesus knew what was happening, so as "great multitudes went with Him" (Luke 14:25a), Jesus chose this moment to lay down some hard criteria for being His disciple—criteria that are critical in the making of a man of God. The Bible says, "He turned and said to them, 'If anyone comes to Me and does not hate his father and mother, wife and children, brothers and sisters, yes, and his own life also, he cannot be My disciple'" (vv. 25b-26).

Now that's a hard saying that would blow some guys right out of the pew. But Jesus wasn't teaching hatred for our family. He was using a language technique to say that our love and devotion for Him has to be far above any human relationship. So far above, in fact, that when we compare our love for Christ with any human love, the latter seems like hate. It's the *comparison* that Jesus was interested in here. He was simply saying that not even the most wonderful and intimate human relationships can come before our devotion to Him if we are going to be His disciples.

### We Must Carry Our Cross to Truly Follow Jesus

I can imagine the looks on the faces of Jesus' listeners after this opening statement. But Jesus was just getting started. "And whoever does not bear his cross and come after Me cannot be My disciple" (Luke 14:27).

Jesus' listeners must have been scratching their heads and looking at each other in disbelief. I can hear one of them whispering to another, "What is He saying? I thought this was going to be easy. I thought we were going to have all the bread and miracles we needed. I didn't bargain for a cross."

But that's what Jesus said. Carrying a cross in His day meant only one thing: you were on your way to die. The Romans, who had invented crucifixion, ruled Israel at this time. They made a condemned person carry the top beam of his cross to his execution. The people who heard Jesus say this had probably witnessed Roman executions before and knew what kind of radical commitment Jesus was calling for here.

Simply put, to carry your cross is to die with Jesus to your own agenda and plans, and even to your own life. There are believers across the globe dying for Jesus every day, paying the ultimate price to follow Him.

You and I may not be called to give our lives for Jesus, but we are to die for Him nonetheless. Paul said, "I have been crucified with Christ" (Galatians 2:20). He was talking about dying to the things of this world and going hard after Christ in all-out commitment and abandonment of self. That's why Paul could also say his goal was that "Christ will be magnified in my body, whether by life or by death" (Philippians 1:20).

My friend, if you're a dead man as far as this world is concerned, you don't have any plans of your own. If you have died, you don't own anything. Your earthly relationships change when you die. The only thing that ultimately matters to a man of God is his relationship to his Master.

Today, however, Jesus' call to bear our cross has largely been reduced to the idea of bearing up under a trial, an illness, or some difficult person or circumstance. But your wife or your children are not your cross—and you're not your wife's cross, either. Neither is your impossible boss your cross to bear, or that old back injury from playing football that keeps you awake in pain some nights. Your cross and mine is the cross of Jesus Christ, which calls us to die daily for Him. Interestingly enough, that's exactly what Paul said: "I die daily" (1 Corinthians 15:31).

## We Must Count the Cost to Be Jesus' Disciple

Now you may be saying, "I'm supposed to count all my human relationships as hate compared to my love for Jesus, and take up my cross to die with Him? Whoa, I need to think about that."

Okay, that's fair. Jesus challenged His listeners in Luke 14 to consider very carefully what they were getting into. He did this by means of two illustrations:

> For which of you, intending to build a tower, does not sit down first and count the cost, whether he has enough to finish it— lest, after he has laid the foundation, and is not able to finish, all who see it begin to mock him, saying, "This man began to build and was not able to finish." Or what king, going to make war against another king, does not sit down first and consider whether he is able with ten thousand to meet him who comes

against him with twenty thousand? Or else, while the other is still a great way off, he sends a delegation and asks conditions of peace. So likewise, whoever of you does not forsake all that he has cannot be My disciple (vv. 28-33).

These two illustrations are a solid one-two combination of what we need to do as potential disciples before saying we are ready to follow Jesus. The first story has to do with counting the cost, making sure you understand the full price of this deal and are willing to pay it, so you don't bail out on the Lord halfway down the road.

The second illustration of the king about to go to war cautions us not to try and go for a prize that we really don't think we can win. Of course, being Jesus' disciple is not a matter of being the biggest, baddest, or strongest guy around. Anyone who follows Jesus faithfully can win this battle. But the point is still made that it's better not to start out on the road to discipleship if you're not wholehearted about giving everything, including your life, to Him.

That's why in verse 33 Jesus said we need to "forsake all" to follow Him. Forsaking all doesn't mean that we're all to take a vow of poverty, sell all of our possessions, and enter a monastery. But it does mean we surrender the ownership of everything we have so that the Master is in control. It's all right to have possessions, as long as Christ possesses your possessions and they don't possess you.

This is the real stuff for people who want to be real Christians. Three times in this passage, Jesus used the phrase "cannot be My disciple." He was laying down the conditions for true discipleship, and He didn't apologize.

I've written this book because I believe there are many men who are tired of being half-hearted, on-again, off-again Christians who can say little else about their spiritual lives except that they know they are going to heaven when they die. But you need to know there is a cost to following Jesus. If you and I want to be Jesus' disciples, we have to move out from the crowd, step over the line, and commit ourselves to Him.

## YOU NEED TO SEE WHERE YOU ARE AS
## JESUS' FOLLOWER, AND MOVE ON FROM THERE

The problem in many of our churches today is that Jesus has too many "fair-weather" friends. You know what a fair-weather friend is. He's the guy who is your buddy, your pal, as long as everything is going great and there's something in it for him. But when times get tough, fair-weather friends disappear like the sunshine on a cloudy day.

It reminds me of a joke that was going around when I was a kid. The Lone Ranger and his faithful Indian companion, Tonto, were riding through the Old West one day when they suddenly looked up and saw hostile Indians coming toward them from every direction. The Lone Ranger turned to Tonto and said grimly, "Looks like we're in big trouble, faithful companion."

Tonto answered, "What you mean 'we,' white man?"

That's a fair-weather friend. You reach out to him in the darkness, but he's not there. I'm afraid a lot of people who claim to follow Jesus do so only as long as they're in the mood, or it doesn't get too demanding. There are three basic kinds of followers of Christ; I want to help you decide where you are today, and then challenge you to move on for the Lord.

### If You're Merely Curious,
### Take the Next Step Forward

The first kind of follower is the curious. These are the people who follow at a distance. They may be intrigued by Jesus and what He teaches, or know a believer whose walk with Christ is appealing or attractive. But they are not quite ready to step out and be identified.

There is nothing wrong with being curious about Jesus. Nicodemus was curious about the Lord when he came to Jesus by night in John 3. Nicodemus wasn't quite ready to step out into the light and follow Jesus at that point, but later he was at least committed enough to come forward and help with Jesus' burial (John 19:39). We could say that Nicodemus took the next step, which is what I challenge you to do if you're just curious about what following Jesus involves. Consider His claims to be your only hope for forgiveness of sins and eternal life, and put your faith in Him alone for your salvation.

## *If You're Convinced About Jesus, Make a Commitment to Follow Him*

Remember when Jesus fed the five thousand with a few loaves and fishes (Matthew 14:13-21; Mark 6:31-44; Luke 9:11-17; John 6:1-14)? Everyone was excited about this Man who could feed a multitude. It was free food and miracles galore, as far as they could see.

But follow the story in John 6 and you'll see that, by the end of that long chapter, Jesus didn't have any followers left except the Twelve. That's because He talked about blood, sacrifice, and commitment. He talked about the demands of discipleship, and all those multitudes turned and went back home.

In fact, things got so rough that Jesus finally turned to the apostles and asked, "Do you also want to go away?" (John 6:67). Peter stepped up and said, "Lord, to whom shall we go? You have the words of eternal life" (v. 68).

Peter and the other apostles had moved from being curious about Jesus to being convinced that He was indeed the Son of God with the message of eternal life (Matthew 16:13-16).

I'm sure the first time Jesus told Peter, Andrew, James, and John to drop their fishing nets and follow Him (Matthew 4:18-22), they did so out of curiosity. Same thing for the tax collector Matthew when Jesus first called him (Mark 2:14). There was something attractive and wonderful about this Man, and they just had to follow Him. Of course, the Holy Spirit was working in their hearts, but I still believe there was a strong element of curiosity in their response. But somewhere along the way, the disciples' curiosity changed to conviction. They were convinced that Jesus was for real, and they were going to stick close to Him.

As a pastor, I meet a lot of men who are convinced that Jesus is the Son of God who is worthy of their devotion, and they can testify to having received Him as their Savior. But they just can't "pull the trigger" and sell out completely to Him. Are you convinced that Jesus is worthy of your complete life and devotion? Praise God! You're a candidate for the next step, which I hope you'll take.

### If You're Committed to Jesus, Keep on Going!

This is the stage we all need to get to as Christian men: the company of the committed. These are the guys who are flat-out for Jesus Christ.

Now if you feel that this is a level of discipleship you can't attain, let me encourage you with the apostles' example. I don't think they really "got it" until after Jesus had risen from the dead and they saw Him. For all of their conviction about Jesus, they all ran off in the Garden of Gethsemane when Jesus was arrested. "Then all the disciples forsook Him and fled," Matthew confessed about himself and the others (Matthew 26:56).

And then, of course, there were Peter's three denials. But Jesus didn't give up on His men. John 21:1-22 is the great story of Peter's restoration after Jesus' resurrection. Then in the book of Acts, we discover that the apostles finally got it and went out to give their lives proclaiming the gospel.

Jesus had told the Twelve earlier, "If anyone desires to come after Me, let him deny himself, and take up his cross daily, and follow Me. For whoever desires to save his life will lose it, but whoever loses his life for My sake will save it" (Luke 9:23-24). They didn't understand what kind of commitment it would take to fulfill Jesus' calling, but they eventually moved from being curious and convinced to being committed.

## CHECK OUT THIS PLAN TO MOVE
## FROM BEING CURIOUS TO BEING COMMITTED

It's exciting to see how the apostles came on so strong and turned the world upside down for Christ. But what about you and me today? What will it take for us to go from being merely curious or convinced about Jesus to being totally committed to Him? How can we move from cold orthodoxy to a burning commitment to Christ? Let me suggest a biblical blueprint drawn from Luke 9:23-24.

### *Being Committed to Jesus Starts with Denying Yourself*

Self-denial is essential for a disciple of Jesus. I know this flies in the face of our self-love culture with its worship of beauty and wealth and ease. Even in the church we have people telling us that we'll never be able to get our Christian act together until we achieve a high self-image and sense of self-worth.

Many of these people are well-meaning, and yes, God did so love the world that He sent Jesus to redeem us. But the Scripture never commands us to love ourselves. Jesus assumed our self-interest when He told us to love our neighbor as ourselves (Matthew 22:39). But that's a far cry from commanding self-love.

Instead, the Bible calls us to abandon ourselves to Jesus. Paul warned us not to think more highly of ourselves than we ought to think (Romans 12:3). And here is Jesus saying, "Deny yourself."

Self-denial means that instead of asking, "What's in this for me?" or "How is this going to affect my career and my comfort?" we say to God, "Not my will, but Yours be done." Self-denial means that we judge ourselves in light of Scripture and deal swiftly and radically with any sin or rebellion the Holy Spirit shows us.

The apostle Paul wrote to the believers in Corinth, "If we would judge ourselves, we would not be judged" (1 Corinthians 11:31). Men who are full of themselves seldom take time to judge themselves, especially in light of the cross.

Now in case you're wondering, denying yourself doesn't mean

walking around with a hang-dog look on your face like you just lost your last friend. Nor does it mean always putting yourself down. Both of those responses are self-focused. Denying yourself has more to do with forgetting about yourself and giving up the right to be and do whatever you want.

What I'm describing is an essential spiritual discipline, just like prayer or fasting. Discipline is seldom easy, and the results we want don't happen overnight. It takes consistent obedience over a long period to become focused, fruitful disciples. If we are going to follow Jesus, we should have no greater pursuit than to know and love Him.

## Being Committed to Jesus
## Means Taking Up Your Cross

We have talked about what it means to "take up [our] cross daily," as Jesus called us to do in Luke 9:23. We said our cross is often misunderstood as some trial we have to bear instead of the instrument by which we die to self. The purpose of the cross is also misunderstood and, I think, weakened somewhat when we make it simply a piece of jewelry or a decoration.

Now if you wear a cross, I'm not saying get rid of it. My wedding ring has a cross on it to remind me of the two most important commitments in my life, my commitment to Jesus Christ, and my commitment to my wife. I wear this ring as a perpetual symbol and reminder to myself of who Jesus is and what my relationship with my wife should be about.

But we need to remember that the cross of Jesus Christ is not an attractive symbol. It was a cruel instrument of death, the ultimate sacrifice. Again, a man who took up his cross was on his way to die—and yet, we are called to take up our cross each day. But it's in dying to self and the world that we come truly alive, because then we are alive to God. One of the ironies of the Christian life is that the way to truly live is to die, because if you try to hang on to your life, you will lose it. But when you surrender your life to God, you find it.

*Being Committed to Jesus Means Following Him*

The last part of Jesus' call in Luke 9:23 was simply, "Follow Me." This pretty much brings us full circle in this business of letting the Master take control of our lives.

I hope it's not a shock to you if I tell you that when you really begin following Jesus, there will be times when you are not happy. Following Jesus may mean forsaking some relationships with people who aren't walking the same way you're walking and are having a negative influence on you. Following Jesus may mean persecution from those who don't like the path you're taking, and it definitely means forsaking the sins that weigh you down along the path (Hebrews 12:1).

The call to follow Jesus is really pretty uncomplicated: deny, take up, and follow. Are you ready for the challenge of letting the Master take charge? Let's go for it!

# 3

# THE IMPORTANCE OF A MAN'S LIFESTYLE

THE STORY IS TOLD OF A Christian young man who received his military draft notice and was facing induction into the army.

The young man's father, who had been a soldier himself, knew his son would face ridicule, harassment, and persecution for being a Christian in the rough world of an army barracks. Dad wanted to prepare his son for army life, so just before the young man left for boot camp, his dad told him about the trials he might have to face as a Christian.

The young man went off with great fear and trembling. After he had been in basic training for a few weeks, he got a letter from his father asking him how things were going and what he had experienced as a Christian.

"Things are going great, Dad!" the young soldier wrote back. "I haven't had any trouble at all. Fortunately, no one has found out yet that I'm a Christian!"

I'm not sure what conditions that young Christian soldier was facing in his army unit, but it's safe to say he was deficient in his understanding of what it means for a Christian to impact the world around him, as Jesus called us to do. We're learning more about what it means to be a man of God who is a growing and developing disciple of Jesus Christ. In Matthew 5:13-16, part of His Sermon on the Mount, Jesus used two powerful word pictures to describe what our lifestyle should look like and the impact He wants us to have as His followers and members of His body, the church.

We have an incredible opportunity today as Christian men to really impact our culture for Jesus Christ. Our wives and children, our coworkers, our friends, and the larger culture are crying out for something—and some*one*—who's real, someone whom they can believe in and follow. I believe we have a special "Kingdom moment" today to make a lasting difference for the Lord.

That's why I was struck by these words from Winston Churchill: "To each there comes in their lifetime a special moment when they are figuratively tapped on the shoulder and offered the chance to do a very special thing, unique to them and fitted to their talents. What a tragedy if that moment finds them unprepared and unqualified for that which could have been their finest hour."

What a challenge that is to me. I want to be spiritually prepared and qualified for this time in which we live. Jesus gave us two timeless illustrations of what it means to be ready for maximum impact when He said, "You are the salt of the earth. . . . You are the light of the world" (Matthew 5:13-14). Jesus used these two common substances to tell us how we, as men of God, are to engage our culture and maximize our impact for Him.

Jesus needs men who are willing to be salt and light because the world is a decaying and dark place. When I was a boy growing up in the First Baptist Church of Conway, Arkansas, some of my fondest memories were being part of what was called the "Sunbeam Band." We used to sing, "A sunbeam I will be, a sunbeam I will be. A sunbeam for Jesus, a sunbeam I will be."

That little truth captured my heart and imagination a long time ago, and I have never forgotten what it taught me. I understood that even though I might be just a little sunbeam or a small pinch of salt, my life could count for the Lord.

God has called every Christian man to live a lifestyle that influences his world for Christ and makes lost people thirsty and hungry to know the Jesus he knows. We are living in a time when it appears that people are inventing new ways to display their sinful depravity. We see the decay now more than ever. In spite of advances in medicine, technology, and science, humanity is becoming more corrupt and contaminated by sin.

This should not surprise us, because Paul said that in the last days, "Evil men and impostors will grow worse and worse, deceiving and being deceived" (2 Timothy 3:13). Just when we think we have seen or heard it all, something else appears to make evil seem more depraved than we ever thought possible. In the last decade of the twentieth century, there was some sense of optimism in America regarding our future. The economy was strong, and the stock market was soaring. Our national security seemed impregnable—but then came 9/11. We were barely into the twenty-first century when our world exploded, and we haven't even begun to see where this scary new world of international terrorism will take us.

So what are we to do? Some would say the world is going to hell, and there's nothing we can do about it. I strongly disagree! There is something we can and must do about it—for the sake of our own children and grandchildren, and for the sake of the work and witness of Christ. Jesus has already told us how to impact a decaying, dark culture.

## WE NEED TO BE STIMULATING AND PENETRATING AS THE SALT OF THE EARTH

If we're going to make a difference, then we must be different. That's an obvious statement, and yet it seems there is very little difference between the way professing Christians live today and the way the world lives. For example, our divorce rate is as high as the divorce rate outside the church.

But Peter tells us that God "called [us] out of darkness into His marvelous light" (1 Peter 2:9). And Jesus told us, "Seek first the kingdom of God and His righteousness" (Matthew 6:33). Doing this will make us distinctive, just as we will be distinctive when we truly become salt and light.

When Jesus says "You are the salt of the earth" and "You are the light of the world," the word *you* is in the emphatic position both times. The idea is, "You, yes *you*, you of all people, are to be salt and light." Jesus is saying to us today, "*You*, man of God, be My salt and light." Let's start with salt.

### The Salt of Our Witness Should Penetrate the Culture

Today we use salt on the table, but in Jesus' day it was used very differently. Since there was no refrigeration, salt was used in the ancient world as a preservative. They rubbed salt into meat or fish to keep them from spoiling as they were sold in the market and then taken home. In order to be effective, the salt had to penetrate deeply.

Our faith also needs to penetrate deeply into our culture. Rather than keeping it to ourselves, we need to go public. It isn't easy, because there are powerful and influential forces in the world that would silence us.

"Don't try to push your narrow views on us," they say. "Truth is relative anyway. Who are you to say what is right? Keep your Christianity to yourself. Don't talk about it."

But we cannot ignore the call from Christ to penetrate our world. It's a scary thought to consider what the world would be like without the preservative of God's church, His people. We are told that in the final hours of human history, Jesus will come for His church and take us with Him to heaven. Then, the preserving and protecting agency of God's people will be gone, and hell itself will break loose.

Jesus spoke of a time He called "great tribulation, such as has not been since the beginning of the world until this time, no, nor ever shall be" (Matthew 24:21). Satan will rule, the Antichrist will be in power, and the world will get what it's always wanted—life without God or His people. The Restrainer will one day be removed, as Paul wrote: "The mystery of lawlessness is already at work; only He who now restrains will do so until He is taken out of the way" (2 Thessalonians 2:7).

It's hard to imagine the rapid and complete decay that will set in on earth when the salt of Christian witness is finally removed. This world will rot as fast as a piece of raw meat under a hot sun. But as long as God leaves us here, He wants us to penetrate our decadent times with the salt of godliness.

Improving the schools or electing the right president will not change people's hearts, which is the only way to change the world. Hearts are changed only through the unique, life-changing, and only message of truth—the gospel of Jesus Christ. And if the world is going to hear the gospel proclaimed and see it demonstrated, it will have to be from us.

### The Salt of Our Witness Should Irritate the Culture

Salt stings as well as preserves. You can't rub spiritual salt into the heart and life of a lost person without creating a sense of irritation.

I want to be careful here, because I am not asking you to be an irritating Christian. We have too many of those already. But the truth of the gospel stings when it hits the decay of sin. You don't have to be rude or overbearing in your witness, but you also need to realize that the truth of Christ has to hurt before it can heal.

When I would skin my knee as a kid, if it was really bad my mother came at me with iodine. That stuff was liquid fire, but she would always say, "If it stings and hurts, it helps." I don't know if I ever really believed that, but I do know that the influence of a Christian's salt can sting a wounded world.

### The Salt of Our Witness Should Stimulate the Culture

Salt is a seasoning agent that brings out the flavor and freshness of food. As salt, we are to season and flavor our lives with the joy that Jesus gives us and the grace of God that dwells in our hearts. Salt can sting when it is applied, but when it is applied with love and concern, it can also stimulate a person's spiritual taste buds.

I don't know many people who really love food that is bland, with little or no taste. Most unbelievers don't really want a taste of a bland life that has no flavor to offer. When the bland try to lead the bland, nothing happens and nobody gets excited.

I was at a coffee shop one day when the person in front of me ordered a nonfat, no sugar, decaf drink. I thought to myself, "Why bother? Where's the zip in that?" Sometimes we need to ask the same question of our lives as Christians. There are too many decaffeinated Christians in our world today. But salt will stimulate tastes as it seasons everything it touches.

Whether our salt needs to sting or flavor, we should be touching our world. Whether we are talking about the way salt penetrates, irritates, or stimulates, the common requirement is that salt has to make contact in order to fulfill its purpose.

## We Can Lose Our Saltiness
## by Allowing It to Be Diluted

Jesus had one more important word about salt in Matthew 5:13. He said, "But if the salt loses its flavor, how shall it be seasoned? It is then good for nothing but to be thrown out and trampled underfoot by men."

If we lose our saltiness, we become useless in terms of our influence on the people around us. One way we can lose our salt is by allowing it to be diluted or mixed with the things of the world. Getting sidetracked by the distractions of life will weaken your witness.

Diluted salt was discarded, tossed out the door to be compacted and walked on by everybody. We have seen some unforgettable examples of very public Christians who have allowed their lives to be polluted by the world, and their testimony and impact for Christ were compromised.

## We Can Lose Our Saltiness
## by Containment in the Shaker

Perhaps the most common way we lose our "saltiness" is simply by keeping the salt of our influence bottled up in the saltshaker. We can do this individually, as in the case of the young soldier I told you about at the beginning of the chapter. We can also do this corporately when we keep our Christianity bottled up behind the doors of our churches.

Our churches are saltshakers in that they are where the salt is gathered. But when we open the doors and go out of the sanctuary, we need to ask God to pour out the salt of our influence into the culture in which we live and work.

## WE NEED TO BE ILLUMINATING AS THE LIGHT OF THE WORLD

We said above that Jesus was also emphatic about the impact of our lifestyle when He changed the illustration to light. "*You* are the light of the world" (Matthew 5:14, emphasis added). Light illuminates, and it dispels darkness. We have a mission from Christ to light up a dark world. How are we to do that?

### We Are to Shine a Conspicuous Light

Jesus went on to explain how we can be a light that shines through the darkness. "A city that is set on a hill cannot be hidden. Nor do they light a lamp and put it under a basket, but on a lampstand, and it gives light to all who are in the house" (vv. 14b-15). In His day, the little towns and villages of Israel, glowing with the lights of many lamps, must have been a welcome sight to a traveler going along in pitch darkness.

Have you ever been driving on the interstate late at night, running low on gas and wondering why you didn't stop for the night at that last town you came through? Then you know the scary feeling that comes over you as you pass mile after mile either of nothing, or of dark, closed-up gas stations.

But when you finally top a hill and see a small light glimmering in the distance, you begin to breathe easier. Even before you know for sure that it's an open gas station, just the presence of that light brings relief and new hope.

Light has that kind of power when it is shining in the darkness. One reason we are to be conspicuous in our witness is that many people who are stumbling around in spiritual darkness are scared to death and are looking for someone with the light. And even those who don't realize that they are walking in darkness need someone to shine the light of Christ on their path. There was a clever television commercial some years ago that showed a person looking out at his dark backyard. He couldn't see anything until he turned on the light to reveal a yard full of terrible monsters in the dark. The punch line of the commercial was that you needed a particular outdoor lighting system because you never know what's out there.

Jesus said, "I am the light of the world" (John 8:12). But He also said *we* are the light of the world. Here's the connection that gets the light of Jesus Christ into our lives and onto our faces: "For it is the God who commanded light to shine out of darkness, who has shone in our hearts to give the light of the knowledge of the glory of God in the face of Jesus Christ" (2 Corinthians 4:6).

When we bathe our hearts in the presence of our King, the glow of His presence and the character of His life are formed in us, and people will see the love and light of our Savior in us.

## We Are to Shine a Consistent Light

If we are to be light in a dark culture we must also be consistent. "Let your light so shine before men, that they may see your good works and glorify your Father in heaven" (Matthew 5:16). Jesus wasn't saying our light has to be perfect, just consistent so that the world would see it and be drawn to Him.

When war in Iraq began in 2003, I wrote our Southern Baptist chaplains to let them know we were praying for them. Our chaplains were there in the battle, shining for Jesus and seasoning the culture around them.

I will never forget the story of Private James Keil, who was baptized in the desert. Bottled water was poured into a hole in the ground as Private Keil professed his faith in Christ and was baptized by a chaplain. Not long after, Private Keil and the maintenance group he was a part of turned the wrong way and were ambushed. James Keil went out into eternity that night, but he died as a believer because faithful chaplains were there sharing the love, hope, and gospel of Jesus.

Someone said a long time ago that it's better to light a candle than to curse the darkness. The best way to dispel darkness is not by shouting against it, but to drive it away by letting our light shine conspicuously and consistently.

## We Are to Shine a Compelling Light

A light brings welcome and warmth, and it shows the way out of a dark place. That's why we're to shine in the darkness. The dying words of O. Henry, the famed short story writer, were, "Turn on the light. I don't want to go home in the dark."

How many people in our world are saying, "Turn on the light. I don't want to go home in the dark"? We must be compelling in shining our light, which means we need to tell people the truth and show them a Christianity that is full-bodied, well-rounded, robust, and worthy of their life's commitment. The church of Jesus Christ is not a club or a resort where people come to relax and bask in the sun to get a good tan so they can go home looking good. The church is a lighthouse warning people away from a dark and dangerous shore on which they will shipwreck their lives.

You may respond, "Well, my life really isn't that compelling. My light is pretty small."

You may not feel compelling—but your light does not come from you anyway. It comes from Christ within you, and He is very compelling. Oswald Chambers, the great devotional writer, said, "Never allow the thought that I'm of no use where I am; you certainly are of no use where you're not."

## We Are to Shine a Consuming Light

Just as a candle burns and consumes itself, we are to be consumed in shining and sharing the light of Jesus Christ.

Now don't misunderstand. I'm not talking about burning yourself out with frenzied activity or overcommitment. But sometimes

I think the church has put so much emphasis on *not* burning our-selves out that we forget to burn at all. I wrote this book to call men of God to "max out" for Him. This is not the time for wimpy, tasteless, dim Christianity. No man I know wants to follow a leader who says, "Follow me into mediocrity!"

There are plenty of people who want to serve God, but only in an advisory capacity. Too many people are the like the guy who spent his days in his hammock in the backyard. When his wife asked him if he was going to get a job, he said, "Yes, but I'm wait-ing for something in upper management."

Shining our light for Jesus Christ is to be our magnificent obsession and our all-consuming passion. A candle is a perfect metaphor for our light, because it burns steadily and consistently for as long as it has life. We are not chandeliers to hang in the foyer of the church sanctuary or over the dining room table to beautify the premises. We're more like a porch light showing people the way home and inviting them to come in.

So the question is, will you apply the salt of an authentic Christian lifestyle and witness to a decaying culture, and let your light shine as you attract people to Jesus? I hope so!

## YOUR SALT WILL TASTE BEST AND YOUR LIGHT WILL SHINE BRIGHTEST THROUGH THE CHURCH

We can't examine a man of God's lifestyle and commitment to be salt and light without talking about the importance of the church in our lives. I have a deep passion for the church of Jesus Christ and the irreplaceable part it must have in the life of the man of God. If you want to be at your saltiest and your brightest for Christ, you need to be radically and irrevocably committed to full participation in a local church.

My love for and commitment to the church did not begin when I became a pastor. I started going to church nine months before I was born, and I never stopped because I have always loved the church and always will. The reasons I want to give you below for being committed to the church have nothing to do with my being a pastor and everything to do with having the same love for the church that Jesus Himself had—and still has!

I am so passionate about the church not only because it's what Jesus was passionate about, but because the church is being sold short today by the American disease of "Me-ism." This affliction causes its victims to think the only thing that matters is me and my individual needs and experiences. This disease has infected Christendom as a whole, and many who claim to be Bible-believing Christians have also caught it.

But let me tell you something. The people of God are not free-floating individuals. We are knitted together as one body in the church the way our bodies are knitted together. This modern emphasis on a personal relationship with Christ at the expense of connectedness to the church is totally contrary to the teaching and example of Christ.

I encourage you to jot down the seven reasons I am about to give you and put them in your Bible so you can remind yourself regularly why you, as the spiritual leader in your home, should make the church a priority for you and your family.

## We Should Be Committed to the Church Out of Loving Obedience

Jesus said, "If you love Me, keep My commandments" (John 14:15). And in Hebrews 10:24-25 the Scripture says, "Let us consider one another in order to stir up love and good works, not forsaking the assembling of ourselves together, as is the manner of some, but exhorting one another, and so much the more as you see the Day approaching."

The Word of God is filled with both exhortations and examples of why membership and participation in the local church is not an option for us as believers. Going to church is not a matter of looking good or scoring points. It's a matter of Christian obedience. And the later it gets in terms of the end times, the stronger our commitment to assemble together should be. The Bible says don't give up on the church!

You can make the case from Scripture that an un-baptized Christian was unheard-of in the church of the New Testament. The same is true of a Christian who gave no thought to the importance of the church, or who bounced around from one church to another without settling down and becoming involved anywhere.

We hear people talk about the "unchurched" today. But a Christian living independently of the church was absolutely a foreign concept to the writers of the New Testament. Can you imagine Paul writing a New Testament epistle "to Joe, my brother in Galatia who doesn't go to church because he says a man can be a Christian without going to church"? No way!

The early church was so serious about membership in a local body that when believers went from one place to another, the church sent letters of introduction and commendation with them so the church in the new city would plug them into the work of that church (see Acts 18:27; Romans 16:1; Colossians 4:10).

I heard about a man who was asked by a friend why he wasn't going to church. "We've been going to church for years, so we decided that we would just take a vacation from church."

Try skipping work next week and then telling your boss when he calls to see why you didn't show up, "You know, I've been working for years, but I just got tired of going in every day so I'm taking a vacation from work."

No man in his right mind would say that to his boss if he cared at all about his job. But are we saying that to Jesus Christ, the Lord of heaven and earth, about His church that He loves and for which He suffered and died? Let's get serious!

## We Should Be Committed to the Church to Experience Fellowship

We as believers belong together. We were made for fellowship. We need each other, as hard as that is for many men to believe, because we are in a spiritual war. It's bad when a soldier becomes isolated from his unit in enemy territory—and it's even worse when he gets wounded and has no comrade around to get him to the medics so he can get patched up.

You may not think of fellowship as a warfare necessity. Fellowship in the church is often reduced to coffee and dough-nuts in Sunday school or a church potluck. Most Southern Baptists believe you have to bring a casserole to get into heaven! But bib-lical fellowship has little if anything to do with what or where you eat. It is so much more.

The Greek word, *koinonia,* comes from a word meaning "com-mon," or shared. The fellowship we need, and which the church is uniquely designed to provide, is the sharing of a common love and a common life. It means being *together* in the fullest sense of that word.

Now it's true that two brothers in Christ may have fellowship over a cup of coffee. But if all they talk about is sports and the kids, they aren't having real fellowship. Here's a passage that helps us understand the essence of Christian fellowship. The apostle John wrote, "That which we have seen and heard we declare to you, that you also may have fellowship with us; and truly our fellowship is with the Father and with His Son Jesus Christ" (1 John 1:3). Then he wrote that as we walk in the light, "We have fellowship with one another" (v. 7).

How do we have fellowship with God? By chatting about cur-rent events and the weather? No, by pouring out our hearts and sharing with Him our needs, burdens, and praises. It's the same with other believers. Fellowship is sharing our lives, love, worship, and service with each other in the church.

## We Should Be Committed to the Church for Spiritual Leadership

This is one that ought to speak to us as men. Most men either are leaders in some area, or think they can be and ought to be leaders.

The problem is that most of us don't want to be led, because we don't want anyone telling us what to do. We're like former heavy-weight champ Muhammad Ali, who was once told by a flight attendant to buckle his seat belt during a flight. "Superman don't need no seat belt," he snapped.

The attendant shot back, "Superman don't need no *airplane*. Now buckle up."

God has given us pastors and spiritual leaders in the church in order to teach, guide, counsel, and direct the members of Christ's body. We are to bring ourselves under the authority of these leaders. Again in Hebrews, we read, "Remember those who rule over you, who have spoken the word of God to you, whose faith follow, considering the outcome of their conduct" (13:7). And in verse 17, "Obey those who rule over you, and be submissive, for they watch out for your souls, as those who must give account. Let them do so with joy and not with grief, for that would be unprofitable for you."

God has vested spiritual authority in the collective body of leaders He has called to oversee the church. When was the last time you heard about an aberrant cult that was led by a body of elders or other leaders instead of by one authoritarian person who wielded absolute power? A person like this almost always has to leave the church behind to do his thing, because that's the only way he can get away with it without being rebuked, challenged, and corrected.

One reason for the church is so that we do not live independently and rebel against spiritual authority or leadership in our lives. We need the counsel and guidance of the Word of God as it is expounded and applied in the church.

Now let me hasten to add that as a senior pastor, I am also a man under authority. The only authority I have is the authority of God's Word. It's not an authority of position, power, or control. And I have brother ministers and men in my church to whom I am accountable—and I wouldn't have it any other way. No one is exempt from the need for spiritual leadership.

And let me give a tip, brother. Your submission to spiritual authority in the church is the most direct route to having true spiritual authority in your home and in the church itself. A military commander may be able to bark out orders and get people to jump around whether they respect him or not, but your family is not a military unit. And neither is the church. It is a living, breathing body of people who need to be loved, nurtured, instructed in the faith, admonished and corrected when necessary, and guided into full spiritual maturity.

## We Should Be Committed to the Church Because of Our Identity

As a Christian, you are forever identified with Christ and with other believers. You are a "little Christ," which is what the word *Christian* means.

So if you are forever identified with Christ, and Christ has forever committed Himself to His church, what does that say about the relationship you should have to the church? You bear Christ's name because you are His, and the church also bears His name because it is His. So your identity as a believer is intricately bound up with the church.

Are you ashamed to identify with Christ, or with His church? To be in the church is to identify with Jesus Christ. Paul could say, "I am not ashamed of the gospel of Christ" (Romans 1:16).

The Bible says Jesus is not ashamed to call us His brothers (Hebrews 2:11). How then can we be ashamed to identify with Him in the church, to stand with the people of God? Remember, we are going to be in heaven forever with Jesus and every blood-bought member of the true church. I don't want heaven to be ashamed of me because I was ashamed or afraid to reveal my true identity as Jesus' disciple. Instead of shrinking, we are called to identify with Christ in the shame and reproach of the cross (Hebrews 13:13). If you don't want to be with God's people on earth, you're not going to enjoy heaven.

## We Should Be Committed to the Church Out of Loyalty

Loyalty is closely linked to identity. The church is a family, and families stick together. Loyalty is one of my favorite words because the ever-faithful love that God has for us is *chesed* in the Hebrew Old Testament. This word has been translated as "lovingkindness" or simply "love," but it can also be translated as "loyal love."

Loyalty is a trait sorely lacking in much of the church today, because of "me first" thinking. A lot of people take the attitude, "I'm just one person. They won't miss me at church. They have lots of people."

But that's selfish thinking, not loyal thinking. Loyalty says, "I know God is seeking and deserves my worship, and I'm not going to be disloyal to Him. I also want to be loyal to my fellow believers because they are counting on me. Maybe there's someone I can pray for, or a ministry I can help with. I'm not going to leave my brothers and sisters hanging."

It must grieve the heart of God when people are disloyal to His family. Brothers and sisters may fight like cats and dogs, but they will stand side by side when an outsider threatens the family, because they love each other. That's loyalty, and it's another important reason to be committed to the church.

## We Should Be Committed to the Church as Our Place of Ministry

God designed spiritual gifts to function within the life of the church. Turning to Hebrews 10 once again, we are told to "stir up love and good works" among one another (v. 24). One way we do this is by exercising our own spiritual gifts and encouraging other believers to use theirs, "for the edifying [building up] of the body of Christ" (Ephesians 4:12b).

This is close to my heart as a pastor, because the last thing a pastor wants is a church full of people who come to watch the paid professionals do the ministry. Some people have the attitude, "What? You expect me to serve at the church? I thought that's what we paid the preacher for."

No, according to Ephesians 4 my responsibility as a pastor is the "equipping of the saints for the work of ministry" (v. 12a). Of course, I need to be an example to the body of dedicated and loving service, following my Lord, who served others even though He was the King.

A believer with a service mind-set doesn't come to church with the attitude, "Okay, I'm here. You've got an hour to please me with the music and message and make me feel better." A servant comes to give and serve, not just to be served.

We often hear people complain, "I didn't get anything out of the church service today," or, "Church doesn't really do anything for me." But that's not really the issue. The question is, what did you give? Generally, we get out of something what we put into it.

What we put into church is our ministry, our service. Your ministry may not be high-profile, but read on in Ephesians 4 and you'll discover that just like a human body, the body of Christ works properly only when "every part does its share" (v. 16).

No person is left out when it comes to ministry in the body. We have church so that we might be equipped and trained, dedicated and challenged, and stimulated to do good works.

## We Should Be Committed to the Church Because of Our Witness

You may not have thought about the importance of your commitment to church in terms of your witness. What I'm talking about is what your dedicated, loyal membership and involvement—or lack thereof—says to the unbelievers who know you.

Do you want to have an impact for Christ among your unsaved coworkers, friends, and family? If church isn't important enough for you to bother with, or if you just bounce around from place to place, lost people will say, "Don't try to give me something you don't seem to be all that excited about."

A seminary professor once said, "Many people have been vaccinated with a mild enough form of Christianity to ensure that they will never catch the real disease."

This is where the issue of our lifestyle and calling to be salt and light gets real. If you don't have the "real disease" of contagious, all-out commitment to Christ, please don't try to pass it along to someone else. But when you and I are fully committed to worship and serve God, and love each other, in the local church, unbelievers will notice. First Corinthians 14:24-25 speaks of an unbeliever coming to church, being convicted by the dynamic ministry of Christ's body, and turning to Him.

This has happened many times at our church in Plano, Texas. I think of a dear Jewish lady who began attending because she wanted to know why all those people were going to this church. She told me later, "When I heard the worship and saw the faces of the people, I knew I needed Jesus." She received Jesus as her Messiah and was baptized, giving her life to follow Him.

When people who don't know Christ meet people who are alive in Him, and come to church to find out what all the excitement is about, they begin to say, "These people really believe this stuff!" And before long, they start believing it too. You can have an awesome influence as a man of God when you give yourself to the ministry of the church that Jesus loves and died for.

PART TWO

# A MAN OF GOD
## AND
# HIS INTEGRITY

# 4

# FACING A FORK
# IN THE ROAD

I'M A BIG BASEBALL FAN, and one of my favorite characters is Yogi Berra, the legendary former catcher for the New York Yankees.

Yogi is as famous for his use of words as he was for his use of a bat and glove. He was a slashing hitter who has slashed up the English language more than once. One of the great "Yogisms" is this piece of timeless advice: "When you come to a fork in the road, take it."

There is actually a solid truth behind that puzzling piece of wisdom from old Yogi. When we come to a fork in the road of life, we have to go one way or the other. We can't just stand there scratching our heads forever, turn back and pretend the choice doesn't exist, or sit down and wait for someone else to come along and make the choice for us.

The reality is that we are constantly facing forks in the road of our lives—and the road we take at these decisive moments will help to shape our lives, the lives of our family, and ultimately even the future of civilization. It's that important that we learn to recognize the true nature of the choices before us, and then make the right choice. This is the first step toward a life of integrity.

Men today are asked to wear many hats and fill many roles. I am convinced that more men and boys are confused today as to what a man is supposed to be and do than at any time in our history. That's why I want to encourage you to make maximum, nothing-held-back commitment to Jesus Christ the top priority in your life. When you and I are sold out to Him, we can live with the kind of integrity it will take to be a man of God in the twenty-first century.

A life of integrity is forged out of the choices we make every day, whether as fathers and husbands or in the workplace. A lot of dads and husbands have abdicated their roles as men of God who are called to lead their churches and their families in God-honoring ways. As the culture around us continues to deteriorate morally, and as the secular world continues to try and push the church into a little "religious corner," out of sight and out of mind, Christian men are standing at a critical fork or point of decision today, with two roads before them.

One of these roads is broad, well-paved, and easy to follow, with plenty of room for one more traveler. The other road is narrow and looks confining. The broad road is filled with people inviting us to join them, while there are few on the narrow road. This is the way Jesus described life's choices (Matthew 7:13-14). Of course, the foundational choice is our decision to trust and follow Him as Savior and Lord. But life-shaping decisions do not end with our salvation. In fact, for most men this is when some really hard decisions begin because now they have a brand-new orientation and mind-set. But whatever the case, we have to make life-shaping decisions all the time.

## WE MUST DELIBERATELY
## CHOOSE TO TAKE THE NARROW ROAD

Now a lot of men would ask, "Why should I take a narrow, difficult road when this wide, easy road is available to me, and most of my neighbors, coworkers, and buddies are already on it?" Good question. The reason is that Jesus said the broad road leads to destruction, while the narrow road leads to life. It takes a man of real integrity and moral strength to take the narrow road, because Jesus is not calling us to a life of ease as His disciples. He told us the truth about what it would cost to follow Him, but He also told us the truth about what we would gain by becoming His disciples.

Taking the broad road is often the easier choice and the more glitzy-looking of the two roads, which is why so many men today are taking it. The world has been hard at work for a long time lining that road with pleasures and allurements, and all some men can see is clear sailing, with no delays or problems.

## There Are Problems Ahead on the Broad Road

But the world's road reminds me of an infamous freeway in Dallas, called the Lyndon B. Johnson Freeway. It loops around the city and suburbs, and offers many lanes.

But any commuter in Dallas can tell you that taking the LBJ, whether at rush hour or on the weekends, can be a bad decision. It can back up before you know it, and without warning you are sitting in a massive traffic jam with no way out. You're there in the middle lane, and you can feel the frustration growing as the cars inch along.

It's especially frustrating to be stuck in a jam on the LBJ when the Texas heat is beating down on you, you're going nowhere, and the jam extends as far you can see. And it doesn't help when the traffic reporter on the radio tells you the problem is about three miles ahead, and all the exits and side roads are also jammed with people bailing off the freeway. Many a Dallas driver has roared onto the LBJ with everything looking good, only to find very quickly that this broad and inviting road led them straight to "destruction."

Jesus talked about a road like the LBJ Freeway, except that it's a spiritual road running through our hearts. It's broad and expansive and offers what looks like an easy path to get where you want to go.

The problem is that this road appeals to our selfish interests and desires. Many men have decided they're going to be their own bosses and go their own way. As a result, their lives revolve around self, because the reality is that when a man takes the broad road, he is on an ego trip.

Thus, we see men who have decided to live self-centered, self-serving lives. They are on a dogged pursuit of the power and pleasures of the world, a pursuit that does not include God because they took the wrong fork in the road.

But let's admit it. Sometimes it's hard for us to see the real picture because a lot of men who are on this road look great. They are enjoying success in their chosen fields and all the perks that come with it. They are recognized and admired. Their homes are beautiful and their lawns are manicured. Their cars are waxed and waiting in the driveway. But the men who live in the beautiful homes and drive the awesome cars are often falling apart on the inside because their lives are built on sand.

## The Narrow Road Leads Us to True Life

That's why we need to see ourselves and the world around us through God's eyes. Jesus gave us the real deal when He called the crowd and His disciples together one day and said:

> Whoever desires to come after Me, let him deny himself, and take up his cross, and follow Me. For whoever desires to save his life will lose it, but whoever loses his life for My sake and the gospel's will save it. For what will it profit a man if he gains the whole world, and loses his own soul? Or what will a man give in exchange for his soul? (Mark 8:34-37).

I don't want to sound too harsh here, but we have to face the fact that many men are living life at the animal level. I say that because an animal lives for three purposes: self-preservation, self-propagation, and self-gratification. It's tragic when men who have been made in the image of God with the capacity to know, love, and serve Him seek fulfillment in the stuff of the world that is passing away.

Certainly, I know many men who are very successful and prosperous who are also faithful, committed servants of Jesus Christ. What I'm saying is that we cannot make life's crucial decisions based on our wants and ambitions, because Jesus Christ measures life by a different standard, and He is calling us to a different pursuit.

## The Narrow Road Leads to True Victory

Did you notice the save/lose, gain/lose language Jesus used in Mark 8? This is terminology men can identify with, because we are all about winning. God has placed within us a strong drive to provide for, protect, and prove ourselves, and now that we don't have to hunt for our daily food, we seek other outlets for our natural aggressiveness.

Women often complain that we can't do anything without turning it into a competition, and they're probably right. We love to test ourselves, particularly against other men, and we love to win.

But since we were created first and foremost for intimate fellowship with God, we can never be completely satisfied with temporal, temporary victories. There are legions of men who have gained what they went after, but after they got it their victory turned hollow, and now they're wondering what life is all about. These men heard all their lives how they needed to get ahead, and they did. But after they reached the top of the ladder, they looked around and asked, "Is this all there is?"

One of the great statements of this syndrome was made by Muhammad Ali after he had been retired from boxing for some time. His family had splintered, and he was beginning to have the symptoms of Parkinson's disease. In an interview with *Sports Illustrated,* Ali said, "I had the world, and it wasn't nuthin'."

I wish we could have that quote framed and hang it in the den or office of every man in this country. That wasn't a preacher, but the man who before Michael Jordan was the most famous and recognizable athlete in the world. Ali literally won the world in his profession, but the glory didn't last.

We also have a biblical example in King Solomon, the wisest and richest man who ever lived. Solomon had it all to a degree we cannot even conceive of, and yet as his foreign wives and his sensual desires led him away from God (read 1 Kings 11:1-8 and Ecclesiastes 2:1-11), he concluded that life was just "vanity of vanities" (Ecclesiastes 1:2).

That means a big zero! It's another way of saying what Jesus said in Mark 8. He left the questions open-ended, but the answers are clear. What do we gain by winning the world at the cost of our souls? Nothing. And what do we have of sufficient worth to exchange for our souls? Nothing.

Getting the answer to those questions right demands an eternal, spiritual perspective. From the other side of eternity, the answer is obvious—but by then it's too late. We can be sure any lost person in hell would give anything to redeem his soul. That's what the rich man in Luke 16:19-31 wanted to do, but it was too late. We have to make life's decisions, as the old Sunday school chorus said, "with eternity's values in view."

## We Need God's Wisdom to Take the Right Road

Do you feel that you're at a key fork in the road in your life? If not, just hang on, because one is probably just ahead. How do we gain the wisdom Jesus was talking about? How do we learn, once and for all, that losing our life in terms of all-out commitment to Him is the way to save it?

This kind of wisdom comes only from God's Word. That's why I am deeply committed to sharing the Word with men. It's exciting to see how many men in our church have a deep hunger to be men of God. All of us need to immerse ourselves in the Scriptures, and we need resources to help us do that. My prayer is that this book will be a resource for you.

And since men usually respond well to a challenge, I like to give the guys in our men's Bible study something to work on from time to time. I found one interesting exercise in the book *Seasons of a Man's Life,* by Patrick Morley, a man whom God is using to speak to men in this generation.

Morley suggests that we take a piece of paper and write down the year of our birth, then add eighty years to it and write down the date of our death, with a dash in between the two dates. Then he challenges us to focus on that little dash, which represents a normal lifespan, and ask ourselves what we are doing with the short amount of time we have between those two dates. Are the things we're doing adding up to something eternally significant? Are we heading toward fulfillment, or futility?

You may be saying, "Jack, this is heavy stuff. Lighten up a little. Let's talk about the stuff we gain when we come to Christ." I love to talk about that too, because when you follow Jesus you gain everything worth having. We could even say that the cross is a plus sign.

But the Christian life is a subtraction as well as an addition. Jesus said we have to lose our lives in terms of this world before we can save them. Turning to Christ means turning away from sin, self, and the world. We have already seen that it means dying to ourselves every day and taking up our cross to follow Jesus to Calvary.

We often talk about the need to make a decision for Christ, because that's exactly what is involved. It's coming to a decisive point—an unmistakable fork in the road that leads to two totally different destinations—and saying, "I choose Christ, wherever He leads me."

If you've ever been on skis or skates, you know what happens when your feet start taking separate routes. You are going down, because your body cannot go in two directions at once.

Neither can your soul. I'm especially concerned about men who are standing at a critical fork in the road today and deciding they can keep one foot in the world and one in the church. They used to be called Sunday Christians, but you can call them cultural Christians or any other term you want. The result is the same, because when a man tries to take the broad road and the narrow road at the same time, his heart is hopelessly divided, and he winds up being miserable in both worlds.

## You Can Step Up Today and Take the Narrow Road with Christ

My brother, you cannot live in the world and in Christ. You won't get anywhere in either sphere; and more importantly, Jesus will not accept divided loyalty from those who want to be His disciples. The two paths He gave us in Mark 8 are not save/save and gain/gain in terms of being able to enjoy the world's best and His best at the same time. There is a loss that precedes the gain in terms of surrendering the earthly that we may lay hold of the heavenly.

You probably remember the saying, "Finders keepers, losers weepers." But Jesus said, "Keepers weepers, losers finders." When we lose our life in surrender and sacrifice to Christ, we find the joy, power, purpose, and eternal life He has for us.

I'm convinced this is what you want, or you probably wouldn't be reading this book. So let me mention some decisions you can make that will help you as you choose the narrow road.

### Decide You Will Be a Promise Keeper

I'm grateful for the Promise Keepers movement that has helped thousands of men in this generation discover the power and joy of living for Christ. But every man of God needs to decide that he will keep his promises to God and will be His sold-out follower. He also needs to keep his promises to his family, his church, his employer—and even to himself. Keeping our word is at the very heart of a life of integrity.

### Decide You Will Be a Pacesetter

A pacesetter is the guy who is willing to step out from the pack and take responsibility to lead. I'm not really talking about being leaders in the public square so much as taking the lead in our families—making a commitment to be there for our wives and children instead of being at the office or somewhere else when they need us.

Too many men have let their wives assume the spiritual leadership of their homes, but that's not God's plan. I often tell a group of men, "Some of you need to go home and say to your wife and children, 'I'm sorry. I have not been the spiritual leader of this family, but by God's grace and the power of His Holy Spirit, from this day forward I'm going to start leading this family spiritually.'"

Values are *caught* by children more than they are *taught*. Kids can read us like books, and they can tell from the atmosphere of your home what is important to you. That's why I hope your home is filled with the fragrance of Christ as your life is being poured out for Him.

## Decide You Will Be a Prayer Warrior

I could bang the drum here, but there's not a lot that needs to be said. Is prayer an integral, indispensable part of your daily routine? It's safe to say that you will never rise higher spiritually than the level of your prayers.

The Bible says, "Far be it from me that I should sin against the Lord in ceasing to pray for you" (1 Samuel 12:23). If you're too busy to pray, you're too busy! Will your wife and children remember you as a man of prayer?

## Decide You Will Be a Peacemaker

"Blessed are the peacemakers, for they shall be called sons of God," Jesus said in Matthew 5:9. A man of God is a reconciler instead of a fight-starter. Peace begins at home and then radiates out through the church into the community.

We need men who are willing to help mend broken lives, whether in prison ministries, across town, or in their own neighborhoods. Of course, the greatest reconciliation takes place when we introduce people to Jesus Christ. The only way many of the people in our world will ever find out that they can have peace with God through Jesus Christ is if we tell them.

## YOU CAN MAKE MORAL DECISIONS THAT REFLECT SPIRITUAL INTEGRITY

There is one very critical area of a man's personal decision making and integrity that I haven't mentioned yet. This is the area of our moral conduct in relation to sexual purity, in light of the sexual temptation and sin that are all around us.

I'll have a lot more to say about this in the following chapter. But I want to set the stage here—and since I'm giving you steps to keep you moving on the narrow road, let me outline some pathways to purity that I believe will help take you toward faithfulness and away from moral failure.

The time is long past to be silent about the plague of sexual temptation and the rate at which we are losing Christian men to failure in this area. We are being bombarded from every side with the filth of a sex-saturated culture. And with the use of Internet pornography reaching epidemic proportions among men in this country, we have to be in each other's faces, as it were, asking the tough questions and challenging our brothers to stay true to their vows and true to God's Word.

It's different today than it used to be. Most of us can remember the days when morality mattered, even to people who made no profession of faith in Jesus Christ. Sure, sexual misconduct has always been winked at in some circles, but at least those who practiced it hid it for fear of public disapproval. Now it is celebrated. We've gone from separate beds for married couples on old television programs like *I Love Lucy* and *The Dick Van Dyke Show*, to sexual free-for-alls in prime time.

But if there is any area where a man of God proves his mettle, it is in keeping himself pure and undefiled from sexual sin—whether in the body or in the mind. I think lists are helpful, and I'll have more for you in upcoming chapters. Here are those pathways of purity you need to take as you come again and again to that fork in the road and desire to make God-honoring decisions in regard to your morality.

### Accept Your Potential for Moral Failure

There is no immunity to temptation. King David was described in the Bible as a man after God's own heart (Acts 13:22), but you know the sordid story of David's adultery with Bathsheba that started with a single lustful look (2 Samuel 11).

David's grievous sin also resulted in the murder of Bathsheba's husband, Uriah, the death of the child she and David conceived out of wedlock, and a dark cloud of mistrust and murder that hung over David's family and throne for the rest of his life. God forgave David, but the consequences of his sin followed him beyond the grave as the next generation of his family unraveled.

The Scripture says, "Let him who thinks he stands take heed lest he fall" (1 Corinthians 10:12). We must recognize that apart from God, every one of us is a target for the enemy.

A man named Jeff Ray used to teach at Southwestern Baptist Seminary in Fort Worth when I was a student. One day a student asked, "Professor Ray, how old do you have to be before you stop being tempted sexually?"

Professor Ray answered, "Well, I don't know, but it's somewhere past eighty-five," which was his age at the time. If you're still breathing, expect to be tempted.

### Affirm That You Don't Have to Give in to Temptation

Sometimes men rationalize their behavior by saying things like, "Well, God made me with these desires," "Just looking at pictures on the Internet is no big deal," or, "If my wife were meeting my needs, I wouldn't be tempted to look for satisfaction elsewhere."

But we have to realize that a victim mentality is bogus. If a man is a Christian, the Holy Spirit lives within him. A man of God needs to say, "I can do all things through Christ who strengthens me" (Philippians 4:13).

*Aim to Be Morally Pure*

When the Hebrew prophet Daniel was taken captive to Babylon at about seventeen years of age, his Babylonian masters tried to change his culture, his language, and even his diet. He was given food that had been sacrificed to idols. But Daniel 1:8 says, "Daniel purposed in his heart that he would not defile himself with the portion of the king's delicacies."

That is one of my favorite verses in all the Bible. Daniel made a resolution to be obedient to God. What we're talking about isn't just behavior modification, but a resolve in the heart that is backed by the power of God's Word and His Spirit and that is reinforced by making right decisions. That will put some steel in a man's spiritual backbone.

As a young man I resolved to be morally pure. This was a high priority for me, and I give all the glory to God that He enabled me to stay sexually pure even though I grew up with the sexual revolution of the 60s breaking out all around me. And over the years, God has strengthened that resolve.

There is a wonderful program for youth today called True Love Waits. It has helped hundreds of thousands of Christian teenagers stay true to God and come to the marriage altar with a clear conscience before Him and their families.

But let's not get the idea that sexual temptation and the need for purity is just a teen thing. A lot of single men think that once they get married and their sexual desires are being legitimately met, they will be free from temptation.

But nothing could be further from the truth. You and I have to renew our resolve each day to be faithful to our wives and to the Lord. And the good thing is that the more we choose the right, the more we build spiritual muscle and the stronger we become. We're not helpless in this battle.

*Abandon All Bitterness in Your Life*

Hebrews 12:15 speaks of a "root of bitterness" that leads to defilement. Then the writer adds in verse 16, "Lest there be any fornicator," which is related to the Greek word *porneia*, the word for sexual immorality of all kinds that yields our word *pornography*.

What does bitterness have to do with sexual sin? If I allow hurt, whether real or perceived, to turn into bitterness, I start thinking with that victim mentality again. "Poor me, I've been hurt, and I didn't deserve it. So I deserve a little pleasure to make up for this injustice."

A preacher once told me that he thought he deserved a little sexual pleasure because he had worked so hard and had been hurt by some in the church. Again, these are the kinds of rationalizations, or rational-*lies*-ations, that we begin to make when we allow bitterness in any form to eat at our souls.

### Avoid the Flesh in All Areas of Your Life

Romans 13:14 says, "Make no provision for the flesh, to fulfill its lusts." In other words, don't give the devil a stick to hit you with! If you know you are weak in a certain area and you walk into temptation in that area, you're being a fool. You're walking into an ambush. Get yourself out of harm's way.

We may honestly say we would never think of cheating on our wives, but we can still make plenty of provision for the flesh by the things we hear, see, and read. The Bible says, "As [a man] thinks in his heart, so is he" (Proverbs 23:7).

Recalling this verse, one guy said it was a wonder he didn't turn into a girl when he was about sixteen, because that's all he thought about. We need to develop some mental toughness in this area. I've been working on that because I grew up in the television generation when kids were pretty pampered. It's just as tempting for me as it is for the next guy to plop down in front of the TV after a long day and start channel-surfing. It takes mental and spiritual toughness to say to yourself, *No, I'm not going to sit here and do this tonight. I'm going to say no to my flesh.* A man no longer has to make any real effort to find sexual stimuli. The effort comes in removing it from our lives. Almost on a weekly basis I hear about men who are captured by *porneia* on the Internet. This is rapidly becoming the greatest moral crisis in men's lives.

### Abstain from Every Form of Evil

That's why Paul counseled Timothy, "Flee also youthful lusts" (2 Timothy 2:22). Run from it. This is one time you don't want to stand and try to fight. The old King James Version says, "Abstain from all appearance of evil" (1 Thessalonians 5:22). That means every time evil raises its ugly head, get out of there.

I don't go to lunch with any woman but my wife, unless it's in a group. I don't counsel women in my office unless the door is open and my secretary is eight feet away.

You say, "Well, are you that suspicious of women or of yourself?" Not necessarily. I just don't want to give the devil a foothold. As a matter of fact, I run just a little bit scared because I know what I need to do to protect myself.

If a situation looks like trouble, it probably is. But I'm afraid that some men who wouldn't think of walking down the street at night if they saw a gang of thugs lingering under a streetlight will walk into sexually compromising situations with their eyes wide open. Maybe you remember the sergeant on the old television police drama *Hill Street Blues* who would tell the officers going out on their shift, "Be careful out there." That's a good word for a man of God.

Let me also say a word about flirting. Some men love to flirt with women other than their wives. It's a little game they play. But it's dangerous, and it is dishonoring to their wives. Don't tell me women come to you wanting to flirt. I think the truth is that men give off signals that say they are looking. Yes, some women are aggressive; but if you really want to, you can stop that stuff cold. Ask your wife to help you if it's really a problem.

### Abide in the Spirit of God

Confess to God, "I can't do this on my own, but I can do all things because You give me the strength." Don't say you can't, when the Spirit of the Living God within you says you can.

## Arm Yourself with the Word of God

The psalmist asked, "How can a young man cleanse his way? By taking heed according to Your word" (Psalm 119:9).

Philippians 4:8 is a verse that ought to be tattooed backwards on our foreheads so we can read it in the mirror every morning. One of the areas it commands us to meditate on is "whatever things are pure." God has made us so that we can really think about only one thing at a time. That means if I'm thinking the right thing, I can't be thinking the wrong thing. This goes back to our need for mental toughness. Saturate and sanctify your mind with Scripture. If you have to, lay the TV remote on top of your Bible so you'll be reminded to shut down the tube and open up God's renewing, life-giving Word.

Some of us need renewed minds because we've got a lot of dirty pictures on our mental walls. We've seen and done some things that are pasted there and are hard to erase. One of the most insidious things about sexual sin is that it enslaves a person. The most sexual organ in our body is our brain. Someone said sex starts in the kitchen, but it really starts in the mind. But, praise God, His Word can cleanse the mind.

## Affirm the Grace and Forgiveness of God

Praise brings power and leads to victory. The devil departs when we praise God. The next time you are tempted in the area of sex, start praising God. And when you fail, confess your sin to Him and thank Him for the cleansing power of His blood (1 John 1:9).

## Remember That You Must Give an Account to God

You cannot sin indiscriminately and independently of your accountability to God. If you are saved, God won't send you to hell; but you'll feel like hell before it's over, if your life goes up in smoke when tested by fire at the judgment seat of Christ (1 Corinthians 3:13).

We are standing at a critical fork in the road today. The road we take and the decisions we make will determine not only our destiny, but the destiny of our children, grandchildren, and their children. Let's take a stand for integrity and purity in every part of our lives.

# 5

# A Call to
# Moral Purity

I HEARD A GREAT STORY about a man of God whom many of us have admired over the years, Cliff Barrows of the Billy Graham evangelistic team. It is said that whenever Mr. Barrows checks into a hotel, the first thing he does is drape a towel over the television in his room and lay his Bible on top of it.

That's a wonderful practice, and it helps explain why the members of the Graham team have kept their witness and integrity intact for over half a century. I'd like to take that a step further and suggest that maybe Christian men ought to be covering their televisions at home and putting their Bibles on top. I don't know where you are vulnerable to temptation, but I do urge you with all the passion of my soul to do whatever it takes to guard your heart and mind and live a life of moral purity.

I think you will agree with me that it is impossible to be a man of God without making a commitment to faithfulness and purity in refraining from sexual sin, both in our minds and in our bodies.

We know that sexual temptation and failure are a huge problem in the world, but really until the last decade or so it was still a hush-hush issue in the church. That was a shame because it meant that many Christian men had to battle this problem in isolation.

And even today, when there is so much more openness on the subject, some men still struggle alone either because they think no one else has their problem and wouldn't understand, or they are too ashamed to address it, or both. But the explosion in Internet sex trafficking has brought the possibility of explicit sexual temptation into every home—and men are falling for it by the thousands.

However, my purpose in this chapter is not to convince you that men are vulnerable to sexual temptation, or that we live in a culture that is shot through with sexual images and perversion at every level. My purpose is to call you to a higher standard of living—a holy standard of thought and action that will equip you to win the battle against sexual temptation before it ever has a chance to escalate and steal our integrity, our marriages and families, and our effectiveness for the Lord.

## WE CAN GO ON THE SPIRITUAL OFFENSIVE AND WIN OVER SEXUAL TEMPTATION

Nobody ever stated the challenge I want to communicate to you better than the apostle Paul, who wrote to the believers in the sex-saturated city of Corinth, "Beloved, let us cleanse ourselves from all filthiness of the flesh and spirit, perfecting holiness in the fear of God" (2 Corinthians 7:1).

If you ever wondered whether temptation really is every man's battle, there it is in black and white. All of us must put away the sin that wants to pollute both our flesh and our spirit. There are various temptations that men face in their lives, and we have talked about things such as pride and greed. But I think most men would agree that their strongest battle in life has to do with sexual purity.

### It's Not Enough Just to Avoid Sin

We are going to come back to 2 Corinthians, so I'll have more to say about this passage below. But notice that the heart of Paul's challenge is our need to perfect our holiness, not just avoid sin.

In other words, we need to go on the offensive spiritually instead of just living from a defensive position and a defeatist mind-set that says, "Sexual temptation is so powerful, and I'm so weak, that I've got to tread carefully or it's going to get me."

Now please don't misunderstand. We *do* need to be on our guard against sexual temptation. And there are times we need to resist and, if necessary, flee from temptation. But if we ever get the idea that we can't win in this area, that we're just victims waiting to be mugged by Satan, we'll be like the guy who read in the paper about a man being killed when a safe fell on him as he walked down the sidewalk one day. The guy reading the article became so obsessed with the fear of being hit by a falling safe that he began to walk everywhere looking up. One day, he stepped off the curb and plunged into an open manhole.

Walking around in fear is not a strategy for victory. I'm talking about an active, positive commitment to holy living that gives us first-strike capability when the enemy brings in his filth. That's why this chapter is titled "A Call to Moral Purity" instead of simply "A Call to Avoid Sexual Immorality" or something similar.

### God Wants Us to Arm Ourselves with His Word

The overwhelming emphasis of Scripture is on our need to take the initiative and so arm ourselves with the Word and mind of God that the enemy has a hard time finding a weak spot to attack. Here are a couple of examples.

Romans 13:12-14 says, "Let us cast off the works of darkness, and let us put on the armor of light. Let us walk properly, as in the day. . . . Put on the Lord Jesus Christ, and make no provision for the flesh, to fulfill its lusts." Again, Paul wrote, "Walk in [or live by] the Spirit, and you shall not fulfill the lust of the flesh" (Galatians 5:16).

There is a tremendous difference between a parent who is always saying to his child, "Cut it out," "Quit that," "Don't you dare break that," without any instruction, and one who takes the time to say, "Here, son, let me show you how to do that so you won't get hurt or break something." God is interested in our positive purity, if I can use that term, as much as He is in seeing us abstain from evil.

As men of God, we are called to a high standard of conduct that demands far more of us, and is so much more rewarding and fulfilling, than just avoiding the so-called big sins. One concern I have for us as Christian men is that we not fall into the trap of "dumbing down" our commitment, especially in the area of sex, to the point that we justify our secret lusts and sins to ourselves because we aren't acting them out. It's easy to settle for less than holiness in this area of sexual purity, but nothing less than holiness will please God.

So what I want us to do is raise the standard of our sexual conduct to a level of purity in mind, heart, and body. I want us to lead God-honoring lives and not have to look down at our boots when anyone—our wives, our children, our brothers in Christ—look to us for an example of faithful, godly living.

With this challenge before us, I want to give you four truths you can drive into the wall of your mind, so to speak, and hang some things on as you seek to live a life of moral integrity and purity.

Since men like to think in concrete terms and want to know how it works and the steps they need to take, putting the truths of God's Word into a list or some other form for remembering helps me, and I think it will help you too. With that in mind, here are four truths to help you apply the Word, given in the form of an acrostic based on the word P-U-R-E.

## IT'S CRITICAL THAT WE
## PREPARE FOR SPIRITUAL ATTACK

In the previous chapter we read about the devices of the devil. Peter warns that Satan is on the prowl like a lion looking for someone to devour (1 Peter 5:8). He loves to catch us off guard and strike when we are not expecting it. But the Bible doesn't say we have to hide in fear. Instead, we need to be "sober" and "vigilant."

We tell our kids, "Look both ways before you cross the street." We don't do this to try and scare them into never crossing a street, but to prepare them to cross safely. The same is true in the spiritual realm. We don't have to run from Satan, but prepare for him.

Preparation is half the battle in the fight against sexual temptation and failure.

It's like the boxer who said, "If I see a punch coming, I can usually defend against it. It's the punch you never see coming that gets you."

It amazes me how completely the Allies in World War II duped the German army into believing their massive invasion of Europe was going to come somewhere other than the Normandy coast of France. The German commanders didn't find out the truth until their soldiers guarding the beaches of Normandy saw the ships coming and called in the alarm. By then it was too late to rush in the defenses needed to stop the Allies.

We don't have to be caught off guard, because God has already told us who and where concerning the attacks we will face.

Neighborhood crime-watch programs are popular in the Dallas area, as they are in many cities and suburbs. An officer who spoke to one group about home security said, "What you want to do is strengthen the target to make it harder for thieves to break into your home. The truth is that the pros are still going to try, but if you strengthen the target, they'll give up and move on to easier pickings."

That's a great word to us as men. Satan is still going to try, and he will target men who have made an all-out commitment to Jesus as Lord of their lives. But the Bible says that when we fortify our hearts and resist Satan, he moves on.

Brother, we *can* win over sin and the powerful, damaging consequences of sin in our lives. We don't have to be Satan's dopes or his dupes! Don't let Satan suggest to you that you are a hopeless victim in his hands, because you're not.

## It's Critical That We Undo Defiling Associations

We read 2 Corinthians 7:1 above. This verse actually is the conclusion of a powerful section of Scripture that addresses our need for moral purity. Paul began this teaching in 6:14 by saying, "Do not be unequally yoked together with unbelievers. For what fellowship has righteousness with lawlessness? And what communion has light with darkness?" Then verse 17, "'Come out from among them and be separate,' says the Lord. 'Do not touch what is unclean, and I will receive you.'"

Perhaps more than any other issue we will deal with, this is where we need to be absolutely honest with God and with ourselves. Too often Christian men have allowed themselves to become linked with that which is impure and immoral.

## Separate Yourself from Evil and to God

Christians used to talk about separating ourselves from the world. We don't hear a lot about that today, probably because it sounds negative. Well, I don't know how you can read 2 Corinthians 6 and not draw the conclusion that God wants us to pull away from people and situations that are pulling us away from Him.

But biblical separation from the world is positive too. It's not just turning from something that is not good for us, but turning to something that is infinitely better—or rather, turning to Someone who has something infinitely better for us. When we undo any defiling associations, we are turning from sin and the customs and culture of this world to God and His holiness and power for living.

## Our Example Will Have a
## Powerful Effect on Our Family

One thing that will really ring your alarm clock in terms of having the right associations is fatherhood. Many dads have heard their child come out with something shocking at the dinner table that has the other kids saying, "What does that mean?" as Mom goes into cardiac arrest.

Dad tries to keep his cool as he looks at junior and says, "Where in the world did you hear *that!*" And when he finds out that junior got it from the kid next door, Dad is suddenly very interested in undoing his son's unholy associations!

I have a friend who used to tell his son, "I know you have to associate with kids at school, on the team, and even in the church youth group who are not walking with the Lord, and that's fine. They need to see your witness. Just make sure the influence is flowing in the right direction, that they aren't pulling you away from the Lord."

It's one thing for a Christian man to kid himself into thinking it's okay to subscribe to all the movie channels on cable or satellite because he can control it and, besides, he'll just look away during the bad parts in the filthy movies. But it's another thing entirely for this father to catch his teenage son watching the same movies.

There was a story a few years ago of a Mafia member in New York whose wife ragged on him for weeks to do something about their thirteen-year-old son, who was skipping school. Dad didn't really care, but to get his wife off his back he finally, in typical Mafia fashion, threatened his son if he didn't start going to school. But the story said the boy told his dad, "I don't wanna go to school. I wanna be a thief like you."

Now I'll grant you that's not an ordinary example, but that boy was really no different than many others who have said to their dads in words and actions, "I wanna be just like you."

I'll tell you, this is where our commitment to be men of God gets very real and gritty. Let me ask you a question: Would it be fine with you if your son or daughter followed your example in the way they relate to their peers, and particularly to the opposite sex?

## We Can't Afford to Let Our Purity Be Compromised

A man may say, "Okay, I may laugh at the dirty jokes at work, but I don't tell any! And I'll admit I like to flirt a little with the women at the office, but I'm not crude like the other guys. The women know I don't mean anything by it. It's just harmless fun."

Sorry, but God's Word says differently. And so does the experience of many men who have fallen into unholy affairs. Someone has called workplace romance the "new infidelity" in our culture. Think about it. In our fathers' generation, and certainly in our grandfathers' day, there weren't that many women in the workplace. Typically, if an affair were going to develop, it would not have been at the workplace. It would happen to traveling salesmen, or in the neighborhood or among friends. And wherever an affair developed, there was a tremendous social stigma with it.

But not anymore. Today, the workplace is the number one place for married people to meet potential affair partners. And the stigma is definitely gone. Office affairs are the stuff of sitcoms. What can start as "innocent" flirting, or a rendezvous over lunch or a cup of coffee, can quickly escalate into emotional attachment and sexual attraction.

It can happen to any man, especially if his marriage isn't what it should be. Here is this woman at work who is building him up and telling him what a great job he's doing. And all of a sudden, he has a sympathetic female ear, someone who will listen to him and seems so understanding.

I'm not putting women down, because it would take a lot of guts for a woman employee, especially if the man is her boss, to say to him, "Please, sir, I don't want to get involved in your problems at home. You need to work that out with your wife."

Let me give you a pretty hard gut check here, brother. Are you getting more of your emotional needs met at work than you are at home? Do you find yourself looking forward to getting to the office in the morning so you can see and talk to that certain female coworker? Are you spending time alone with another woman, even if it's high noon at a restaurant? If so, you're flirting with disaster! That relationship is Satan's net, and you'd better cut it off now before it snares you. If you can't do it alone, get someone to help you.

### Don't Set Yourself Up for Moral Failure

A guy may say, "Yeah, but you don't know my situation at home. If it weren't for my secretary, I wouldn't be getting any attention or affirmation." Well, if that's truly the case, then instead of taking your secretary out to lunch, take your wife out to dinner and talk about it. If you're going to reach out, reach out to the woman God gave you.

Looking for love in all the wrong places just means that now you have at least two problems on your hands—one at work and one at home. Actually, you have three problems, because God is displeased with unholy associations.

What I'm saying is that following the world's pattern is a sure-fire dead end. When we act like the unbelievers around us, we set ourselves up for moral and spiritual failure.

The question that someone usually asks at this point is, "But doesn't the Bible say we are supposed to go outside the church and our Christian circle to reach out to the world?"

Of course, it does. Paul wasn't telling us to cut off all contact with the world. Being "unequally yoked" refers to the primary associations of our lives—partnerships and relationships that bring us into intimate contact with unbelievers in a way that could silence and compromise our Christian walk and witness. Marriage is usually the first example that comes to mind, but the principle reaches far beyond that.

Check out the Old Testament quotations Paul used in 2 Corinthians 6:16-18 and you'll see that they refer to periods in Israel's life when God's people were being defiled by the idol-worshiping nations around them. As in the example of my friend with his son, the spiritual influence was flowing in the wrong direction. Israel was not bringing its neighbors to the worship of Yahweh, but was adopting their idols and eventually the sexual perversion that went with them.

I hope you're on the alert in your relationships with women besides your wife, to keep those relationships holy and undefiled. How about your computer? If necessary, put a filter on it to screen out pornography before it ever gets to you. Just as you put a seatbelt on when you drive, put a filter on your Internet. And be accountable for the way you use it. Ask your buddy at work or your wife to check you.

Do whatever it takes to *un*do defiling associations. Don't compromise, because the minute you start saying yes to some of the seemingly harmless things, Satan has a foothold. The Bible says don't give Satan a foothold in your life (Ephesians 4:27), because I guarantee you he'll go from a foothold to a chokehold!

## It's Critical That We Remember the Consequences of Sexual Sin

The third letter of our P-U-R-E acrostic is the need to remember that sin always has consequences. Look once more at 2 Corinthians 7:1 and notice Paul said that instead of yoking ourselves together with unbelievers, our calling is to perfect holiness "in the *fear of God*" (emphasis added).

### God's Holiness Demands That He Deal with Sin

I have a healthy fear of Almighty God. He is holy, and He demands holiness of us. The Scripture says, "As He who called you is holy, you also be holy in all your conduct, because it is written, 'Be holy, for I am holy'" (1 Peter 1:15-16). If we dabble in sin, God is going to deal with us and discipline us. Yes, Christ has taken away our sin, and God is a God of love. But He is also perfect purity and righteousness who "will not at all acquit the wicked" (Nahum 1:3). A man of God is one who fears Him.

It's amazing how many men actually think they can cover up sin and dodge the consequences. But we are told in Scripture, "Be sure your sin will find you out" (Numbers 32:23). Remember the consequences of sexual sin: a broken marriage, losing the respect of your children, a possible loss of employment, exposure to disease, the destruction of your witness and testimony for Christ, and the loss of your leadership in the church.

It breaks my heart to say that there are a lot of men who used to be leaders in God's work who are now on the shelf because of compromise and failure in their moral lives. We know that sin can be very attractive, and part of the allure of sexual sin is the promise it holds out of gratifying the desires of the flesh. But the damage lasts a lot longer than any stolen moment of pleasure.

### There Is No Such Thing as a "Free Sin"

I didn't see it, but I remember when the movie *Fatal Attraction* was released. It involved a married man who thought he was indulging in a harmless little fling with another woman until he discovered that the woman was psycho. She began to stalk him until she finally tried to kill him.

That film scared a lot of men straight. There is a bondage and addiction built into sexual sin that begins to feed on a man's body and mind like a cancer. One man who was deep into pornography and sexual sin told his Christian counselor, "I'm so messed up even my perversions have perversions." The nature of sin is always to want a bigger kick, just like a drug addict needs ever-larger and more frequent fixes to get the same reaction. Sexual sin distorts your thinking, defiles your body, disrupts your relationships, and defeats your testimony.

We're talking about the consequences of sin. God can and will forgive sin, but He does not automatically cancel its results. Besides what it does to everyone around you, falling into sexual sin creates a guilt and self-loathing that makes a man barely able to stand living with himself.

I heard this described vividly when I asked a Christian man I knew who had been discovered living a life of immorality, "How could you show up at church every week during that time and act as if nothing were wrong?"

He replied, "Every time I sinned, every time I indulged my fantasies, I would promise God that it would be the last time. I would repent and weep and be broken, only to be defeated again and again."

Anyone who is doing something he doesn't want to do and that he knows is damaging, and yet he cannot stop doing it, is by definition an addict. Maybe the worst consequence of sexual sin is the web it weaves around its victim until he is so tied up he can't even move.

And lest you think I'm being too dramatic, let me suggest that you sit down with a piece of paper and write out every consequence you can think of that would befall you if you indulged in immorality, and list every person who would be affected by your sin and the specific way each person would be impacted. It's a sobering exercise, but one that will help drive you to the Lord pleading for His holiness in your life.

## IT's CRITICAL THAT WE ENGAGE IN POSITIVE SPIRITUAL ACTIVITIES

The fourth and final letter of our P-U-R-E acrostic involves the replacement principle. Instead of just saying no to sin, if you really want to defeat it then fill that place with positive spiritual activities. Here are some suggestions.

### Fortify Your Faith with the Word of God

"Your word I have hidden in my heart, that I might not sin against You" (Psalm 119:11). That's why reading, studying, and memorizing Scripture are so important. If your church doesn't have a men's Bible study, help get one organized. I praise God for literally hundreds of guys at our church who are deeply committed to our men's Bible study. We have seen lives changed.

I said earlier that biblical separation from the world is positive. It's not just separating ourselves from wrong, but joining ourselves to that which is right and wholesome and holy. Make it a point to surround yourself with other men who share your commitment to live holy lives before the Lord. Fortify your faith with the rock-solid foundation of God's Word.

### Purify Your Thought Life

"Do not be conformed to this world, but be transformed by the renewing of your mind" (Romans 12:2). We renew our minds by meditating on holy rather than unholy things.

You know what it's like to tell yourself you are not going to do something, and then grit your teeth and try not to think about it. A person who hopes to eat less and lose weight simply by not thinking about food will think about it all the time. It's not enough just to banish the thoughts we don't want. We need to replace them with the things of God and His Word.

The fact is that you cannot be thinking unholy thoughts if you're thinking holy thoughts. But it requires disciplining your mind.

You say, "That's a hard thing to do." Sure, it is. If it were easy, everybody would do it. But you can do it with the help of the Holy Spirit. Discipline your mind by not indulging fantasies and lies and temptations.

## Identify Accountability Partners

Find someone you can trust and are willing to open up to. For many men, their wives are their primary accountability partners. But it also helps to have another man or small group of men who have your permission to hold you accountable to your commitments. One of the signs of a man heading for trouble is when he begins to avoid his friends and is evasive and noncommittal when he does talk with them. Be accountable to others.

## Magnify the Lord Jesus

We have a greater love than any love on earth, and that is our relationship with Christ. When we allow Jesus to be Lord of our lives, He begins to clean up our minds, our desires, and our actions. When we exalt Christ in our lives, our love for Him will be far greater than our love of sin.

That's what it comes down to. Jesus said the greatest commandment is, "You shall love the Lord your God with all your heart, with all your soul, and with all your mind" (Matthew 22:37).

My brother, there are more important things in life than sex. That may be news to men out there in the world, but as men of God we have to get our thinking straight. At the top of our list of life's priorities is our love for and walk with Jesus Christ. He is the one who calls us to moral purity, and He will give us the power to obey Him so that we become the victor and not the victim in this area.

# 6

# A MAN AND HIS MONEY

PERHAPS YOU HAVE HEARD the story of a man in the construction business who had a promising young employee come to work for him. This young man was bright, sharp, and very talented, and the owner of the company had high hopes for him. In time he even came to regard his young employee as a son and took a very personal interest in him.

So when this young man became engaged, the owner decided to do something special. He told the young man that he was being put in charge of building a very large home, on which no expense was to be spared. The young man had a huge budget and was told to use the finest materials in every detail of the home. The owner also told his young employee that if he did a good job, he would be handsomely rewarded.

The young man set to work. But sadly, even though he was smart and talented, he loved money more than anything else, including his personal integrity. So it wasn't long before his greed took over. He began to build the house with inferior materials at every stage of the building, while still making sure the outside of the house looked good. Then he would bill the company for top-quality materials and pocket the difference.

He figured no one would catch on to his scheme since he was the boss on the project. He also assumed that by the time the house's flaws showed up, he wouldn't be around. This dishonest young man congratulated himself on being able to pocket all that extra money, which he figured would give him a great start in his married life. He also eagerly anticipated his reward from the owner when the house was finished.

That day arrived, and the owner came to see the finished product. The house looked great, even though it had serious flaws and weaknesses. The owner said to his young friend, "You have indeed built a beautiful house. My reward to you is to give this house to you and your future bride as my wedding present."

The young man was stunned as he realized what a fool he had been to let his greed get the better of him. But he dared not object or say anything to his boss, or his dishonesty would be discovered. He was also deeply chagrined to realize how much his boss cared about him and trusted him, and how terribly he had treated that trust. So the greedy young man, now sadder but much wiser, moved his new bride into a home that he knew would soon be crumbling around them.

I don't know if that story is true or apocryphal, but it's a great illustration of the need for integrity in the way we handle money. This young man's dishonesty as a manager reminds me of Jesus' words in Luke 16: "If you have not been faithful in the unrighteous mammon, who will commit to your trust the true riches? And if you have not been faithful in what is another man's, who will give you what is your own?" (vv. 11-12). This came after the parable of the dishonest manager, or steward, who had squandered his master's property (vv. 1-8).

It's time to talk about money—a subject that interests all of us. In fact, I wonder about someone who says he is not interested in money, because Jesus was very interested in it. He knew that no area of life reveals the state of our hearts more readily than our attitude toward money and the things it can buy. Jesus' parables and other teachings reveal the attention He gave to money and, by extension, material possessions. Sixteen of our Lord's thirty-eight parables deal with money and the responsibilities associated with it. Overall, Jesus said far more in the Gospels about money and material possessions than He said about prayer, heaven, and hell put together.

The operative terms the Bible uses for our management of God's money are "steward" and "stewardship." This word in its various forms refers to a manager, someone who in Jesus' day did not own the estate on which he lived but simply managed it and its finances for the owner.

Stewards in biblical days were often entrusted with great wealth to manage. And as the parable in Luke 16 makes clear, an owner could call for a full accounting from his steward anytime he wished. That's why so much of Jesus' teaching on money includes a strong element of responsibility and wise management on our part as stewards of what God has entrusted to us.

I like the description of stewardship as that area of life in which men make money, and God makes men. I believe God wants to prosper His people. Now before you begin "naming and claiming" everything you want from God, I want to be sure you know I am not promoting the "health-and-wealth" gospel that is so popular in some Christian circles today. It is clearly not God's will that every Christian be healthy and/or wealthy, but I do believe it is His plan that we prosper in accordance with His Word. Consider these Scriptures:

"He [the righteous man] shall be like a tree planted by the rivers of water, that brings forth its fruit in its season, whose leaf also shall not wither; and whatever he does shall prosper" (Psalm 1:3).

Joshua 1:8 is one of my favorite Scriptures: "This Book of the Law shall not depart from your mouth, but you shall meditate in it day and night, that you may observe to do according to all that is written in it. For then you will make your way prosperous, and then you will have good success."

We also read, "I pray that you may prosper in all things and be in health, just as your soul prospers" (3 John 2).

God's will is that we prosper as men of God. But that doesn't mean we're going to be fat cats, living high, wide, and handsome, as they used to say. Prosperity from a biblical standpoint is rarely measured in financial or material terms alone. It has more to do with the ability to enjoy what God gives than with how much He gives.

A man of God can be content even with comparatively little of the world's goods, because he understands that his true worth is not in his bank account.

## WE NEED TO GET OUR THINKING STRAIGHT ABOUT THE MONEY GOD ENTRUSTS TO US

But the fact remains that money is an important part of our lives. It is still the medium of exchange in our culture, and it is one of the tools God gives us to meet our needs and build His Kingdom. Our attitude toward money also helps reveal the condition of our hearts, which is why Jesus said, "Where your treasure is, there your heart will be also" (Matthew 6:21).

So our responsibility to handle money in godly and wise ways is inescapable—making it crucial that we get our attitude toward money straight. Here are some biblical ways to think about the money God gives us as His stewards or managers.

### Everything We Think We Have Really Belongs to God

I stated it this way because as far as heaven is concerned, what we call ownership on earth is really just "loanership." What we have is on loan to us from God. It all belongs to Him—all of it!

Don't think of your life as a pie that you slice up so that you can give God the slice that belongs to Him. For instance, some men cut their days into seven slices, keeping six for themselves and giving one day to God as if that's all He requires of our time. But all of our minutes and hours belong to God. So does our money (we'll discuss giving below).

The Bible declares, "The earth is the LORD's, and all its fullness, the world and those who dwell therein" (Psalm 24:1). God said through the prophet, "The silver is Mine, and the gold is Mine" (Haggai 2:8). Everything belongs to God.

### *God Wants Us to Be*
### *Content with What He Gives Us*

One great attitude check you and I can take anytime is to measure our level of contentment with what God has provided.

Contentment is a big deal to God, because a lack of it reveals a heart of greed and tells God that we don't think He is being as good to us as we deserve. That's why the Bible says, "Godliness with contentment is great gain" (1 Timothy 6:6).

Paul then added, "Having food and clothing, with these we shall be content. But those who desire to be rich fall into temptation and a snare" (vv. 8-9a).

### *God Wants Us to Understand Our True Net Worth*

Would you like to know your net worth? Then add up everything you have that money can't buy and death can't take away, and that is your true net worth. It is the sum total of everything God has given you that will still have value in eternity. And in that realm, you are as rich as Jesus Christ because God has blessed you "with every spiritual blessing in the heavenly places in Christ" (Ephesians 1:3).

I'm wealthy because I have a wonderful family, I was privileged to grow up in a great home, and I am able to serve God in the fellowship of His church. I am rich because I have the inerrant, infallible, and life-changing Word of God. I am immensely wealthy in friends in the family of faith who encourage and strengthen me and my family.

### *We Need to Be Grateful for What God Gives Us*

Did you know that one of the unfailing marks of a Christian is gratitude? If you want an interesting study, get a Bible concordance (a study tool I highly recommend you add to your library) and look up words like *gratitude, grateful,* and *thanks* in the New Testament.

One verse you'll discover is Ephesians 5:20, which says that the mind-set God wants us to have includes "giving thanks always for all things to God the Father in the name of our Lord Jesus

Christ." Those "all things" include the money we have, which means that whether I have a dime or a dollar, I am to be grateful to God because all of my money is a gift from Him.

*We Need to Understand*
*That Our Wealth Is God's Doing*

Deuteronomy 8:18 is a very important verse in any study of biblical stewardship. "You shall remember the LORD your God, for it is He who gives you power to get wealth."

Many men like to think that they made their money all by themselves by their business acumen or savvy investing. Well, we are going to see below that, in fact, hard work and investing are legitimate ways to acquire money. But so-called self-made men need to ask who gave them the mind to think and make those good business decisions or investments. Who gave them the opportunity to be successful? God did.

Ecclesiastes 5:19 says, "As for every man to whom God has given riches and wealth, and given him power to eat of it, to receive his heritage and rejoice in his labor—this is the gift of God." I believe that, as men of God, we ought to look in the mirror each morning and ask ourselves this question: "Who makes you differ from another? And what do you have that you did not receive? Now if you did indeed receive it, why do you boast as if you had not received it?" (1 Corinthians 4:7).

Before we move on, I want to briefly address a question that usually comes up in a study like this. This is the question of believers who have very little in terms of material possessions.

Please know first of all that the Scripture does not teach that wealth is a sure-fire sign of God's blessing, or that poverty is always a sign of God's displeasure. We do not have the insight to explain why one man of God prospers financially while another struggles. Assuming that both men are doing right before God, I have to conclude that their financial condition is one of God's sovereign choices.

I do know God is faithful and wants to bless His people. But that doesn't mean He is going to rain pennies from heaven down on us. Here are three principles for acquiring and handling money in God-honoring ways.

## THE MONEY WE HAVE SHOULD BE RIGHTFULLY GAINED

The Bible is clear that there are right and wrong ways to get money. Sometimes we think that when we talk about money in the church, it's all about giving. But God is also deeply interested in how we get our money. I want to mention some of the ways Scripture forbids us to get money, then look at legitimate ways of acquiring it.

### Stealing Is Prohibited by God's Command

It might seem that there is no need to state the obvious—that God commands His people, "You shall not steal" (Exodus 20:15). But it's good for us to be reminded that God considered stealing so seriously that He included it in the Ten Commandments. And given the temptations and opportunities for fraud and dishonesty that surround so many men today, we need to hear the Word of God again.

A man who was notorious for his ruthlessness in business once said to author Mark Twain, "Before I die, I mean to make a pilgrimage to the Holy Land. I will climb Mount Sinai and read the Ten Commandments aloud at the top."

"I have a better idea," Twain replied. "You could stay home in Boston and keep them."

God forbid that we should be loud in our proclamation of God's Word and then fail to obey it. The Mosaic Law imposed harsh penalties on a thief. "If a man steals an ox or a sheep, and slaughters it or sells it, he shall restore five oxen for an ox and four sheep for a sheep" (Exodus 22:1). That's a principle of restitution that might deter some private and corporate thieves today. Horse thieves were hanged in the Old West because when you stole a man's horse you not only stole his most valued possession, but often his means of making a livelihood.

*Don't Take Money Under False Pretenses*

Another prohibition in Scripture is taking money under false pretenses, or by false representation. Leviticus 19:11 says, "You shall not steal, nor deal falsely, nor lie to one another." This covers a pretty wide range of offenses. In biblical days it involved people who used dishonest weights and measures in their business—which, by the way, was one of the sins the Old Testament prophets warned against and said would bring God's judgment on His people. "Dishonest scales are an abomination to the LORD, but a just weight is His delight" (Proverbs 11:1). In our day we call it the butcher's thumb on the scale.

I heard about a man who ordered 1,000 pounds of stone for some project around his home. When the stone company delivered the order, he decided for some reason to weigh the stones. It turned out that the load was something like 875 pounds, so he called and demanded the rest of the stone he had paid for.

Now I realize it would be hard to weigh out an exact amount when dealing with large stones of various sizes. But the point is still made. If you're going to sell someone 1,000 pounds of something, deliver that amount. If the man could weigh the load, the company could have weighed it.

Gaining money by false representation also includes selling something, such as a car, that we say is in good shape when we know it has problems and is not worth the price we're asking.

Here's one that is very common in the workplace: being on the clock at work, but not working. If you don't give your employer a day's work for a day's pay, that is taking money through falsehood. As men of God, we ought to be the hardest-working guys in the office or on the job.

You may remember a few years ago there was a sudden flurry of résumé fraud by public figures. The one most men remember is the man who was hired as head football coach at Notre Dame, only to be fired when it was learned he had lied on his résumé. Anytime we lie or withhold the truth to make a buck or get ahead, it is an abomination to God.

## Don't Fail to Pay for Work Done for You

Another bogus way to gain money is by nonpayment for work done: "Woe to him who builds his house by unrighteousness and his chambers by injustice, who uses his neighbor's service without wages and gives him nothing for his work" (Jeremiah 22:13).

The Scriptures are so incredibly practical. Jeremiah's warning is as up-to-date as the headlines. We heard of top executives in the Enron company building million-dollar houses and fattening their portfolios while defrauding their workers.

James had a word of warning for employers who refuse to pay their workers: "Indeed the wages of the laborers who mowed your fields, which you kept back by fraud, cry out; and the cries of the reapers have reached the ears of the Lord" (James 5:4). God is keeping His own set of books, and they can't be cooked.

## Don't Charge Other People High Interest Rates

Still another way to improperly make money is to take advantage of people in need by charging exorbitant interest, what the Bible calls usury. The Bible warns against this in numerous places (see Deuteronomy 23:19 for an example).

We could also apply this principle to the practice of charging exorbitant rates for goods or services to people who need them. We've all heard of price-gouging when people were in desperate need of something after, say, a disaster—someone decided to cash in on the situation by charging many times what the goods would normally be worth.

## Don't Borrow Money You Won't or Can't Repay

Here's a final way the Bible forbids us to get money. Some people deliberately dodge and default on a loan that was made to them in good faith. This can apply to formal loans from a lender, but also to money borrowed from family or friends with no real intention of paying it back.

Not surprisingly, God's Word has a pointed word on this issue.

"The wicked borrows and does not repay" (Psalm 37:21). The Bible does not prohibit borrowing at legitimate interest rates, but it is wicked and sinful not to repay a debt.

People often quote Romans 13:8: "Owe no one anything." That doesn't mean we are never to borrow, but it means when the bill comes due, pay it. A more accurate translation would be, "Let no debt remain outstanding" (NIV). This principle also applies to paying our bills for goods and services we have subscribed to. As men of God, integrity demands that we pay our bills. Our credit report should be a credit to the Lord.

## RIGHTFUL WAYS TO GAIN WEALTH

It's amazing how many wrong ways there are to get money. Now let's talk about some right and legitimate ways.

### Inheriting Money Is One Rightful Way to Gain It

The Bible talks a great deal about inheritance. I frankly wasn't blessed with a whole lot of material inheritance, although I had a wonderful spiritual inheritance of a mom and dad who loved the Lord and a family of faith at my church.

Sometimes we look with jaundiced eye at someone who has inherited money, especially if it's a lot. But there's nothing wrong with inheritance. Ezekiel 46:16 says, "If the prince gives a gift of some of his inheritance to any of his sons, it shall belong to his sons; it is their possession by inheritance."

Maybe one of the reasons we look askance at heirs is the story of the prodigal son in Luke 15. This guy had a rotten attitude and wasted his inheritance, but he could still say to his father, "Give me the portion of goods that falls to me" (v. 12), because it was rightfully his.

When John Kennedy was campaigning for the presidency, he stood one day outside a West Virginia coal mine, shaking hands with the miners as they came out with coal-blackened faces. One miner stopped and said to Kennedy, "I understand you've never had to work a day in your life." Kennedy admitted it was true.

"You haven't missed a thing," came back the deadpan answer.

The vast majority of us don't have to worry about having so much inheritance we never have to work. But in case you're one of those rare few who do, you are in a great position to serve the Lord. The late John Kennedy, Jr., said his grandmother Rose would often pull him aside and remind him, "To whom much is given, from him much will be required," referring to Luke 12:48.

The Bible not only condones inheritances, but encourages us to leave something for our families. "A good man leaves an inheritance to his children's children" (Proverbs 13:22).

### Saving Money Is Also a Rightful Way to Gain It

Saving money is also encouraged and taught in Scripture. In fact, the Bible says that a man who spends everything he makes is foolish (see Proverbs 21:20).

One of our biggest problems as Americans is that we are not only spending everything we make, but more than we make. A lot of us need plastic surgery—we need to cut those credit cards out of our lives. The late Christian financial counselor Larry Burkett used to urge Christians to write down a pledge to God that they would quit using their credit cards the first time they had a monthly bill they couldn't pay, then post that promise on their refrigerator as a constant reminder not to fall into the bottomless pit of consumer debt.

I like going to the mall as much as the next person. It's overwhelming here in the suburban Dallas area, as I'm sure it is in many large cities. I see all this stuff and say to myself sometimes, *My goodness, when is enough enough?*

I love the story of the old guy with a lisp who went to New York City and said, "When I went to New York Thity, I thaw a lot of things. But thank God, I didn't thee a thingle thing I wanted." That's an attitude we ought to adopt as men who want to please God. Proverbs 6:6-8 describes how ants are smart enough to save up and store away food while they have the opportunity. I'd like to think we are smarter than ants—wouldn't you? But it would be hard to prove it sometimes by our poor saving habits.

*We Can Also Invest to Rightfully Gain Money*

Investing is one more legitimate way to make money. God has put His stamp of approval on this way of increasing our wealth. Think of Jesus' parables of the talents in Matthew 25 and the minas in Luke 19 (both are sums of money). In each case, the servants who carefully invested their masters' money and made a profit were praised and rewarded.

Now someone will say Jesus was talking about eternal, spiritual investments and rewards, and that's true. But He still used the analogy of financial investment as an example of using our resources wisely as God's stewards.

There is an illegitimate side to investing, which is wild and foolhardy speculation to make a quick killing. A few years ago, the term "day trading" suddenly burst into the news headlines when a day trader in Atlanta snapped and killed several people, including his wife and children, then killed himself. Most of us had never even heard of day trading, but we found out that it is a high-risk, high-stakes gamble that can make or break a person in no time.

We need to stay away from get-rich-quick schemes. What's the old rule of thumb? If it sounds too good to be true, it probably is.

*Hard Work Is Always a*
*Rightful Way to Gain Money*

Most of us fall into the category of those who must work hard for a living. Somebody has said the reason some people don't have money is because it comes dressed in overalls. They're like the guy who said, "Hard work doesn't scare me. I can lie down beside it and go right to sleep."

My father was from the Depression and World War II generation, the one that newscaster Tom Brokaw has called the "greatest generation." The motto of this generation was, "Hard work never killed anybody." The Bible would support that view. Our God is a working God. He created the heavens and the earth, and because we are made in His image, He has given us the capacity to work.

The apostle Paul believed in work. When he heard that some

people in the church at Thessalonica were being lazy and refusing to work, he fired off this "memo": "Even when we were with you, we commanded you this: If anyone will not work, neither shall he eat" (2 Thessalonians 3:10). End of discussion. The Scripture says we are to work for our livelihood, whether we wear a white or blue collar.

## THE MONEY WE HAVE
## SHOULD BE REASONABLY GUARDED

I'm not going to spend too much time on this point, for two reasons. One reason is that I think most men need more help in the areas of how they get and give, or don't give, their money. Second, I'm not a financial or estate planner, so this is not my area of expertise.

### We Need to Guard Our
### Money to Use It for God's Glory

My focus here is more on the importance of guarding what we have so that we can not only meet our own needs, but use our money for God's glory. I read a sad statistic that if the average sixty-five-year-old man in America cashed out, subtracting his debts from his assets, he would be left with one hundred dollars. Isn't it a shame that a man would work his whole life and have so little left? I know we just saw that our true net worth, from a Kingdom standpoint, is spiritual and not material. But that doesn't excuse us from being good stewards of God's money.

I realize some people have little because they have given it all away. But that has to be the rare exception. It is also true that not every man is blessed with great material wealth. But the point of the statistic I quoted is that most people are so deeply in debt that it would eat all but a few dollars of their estate.

For some men, the term "guarding" their money may invoke images of fighting to get it and then fighting to keep it from those who are trying to take it away. But I'm not at all saying that we have to fight and strain and hoard our money in order to guard it.

*Entrust Your Money to the Lord*

In fact, I'm saying just the opposite. The best way to guard our money is to entrust it to the Lord. A lot of people in the Depression generation didn't trust banks. So the stories grew of farmers and others who kept their money under their mattresses or buried in a coffee can in the backyard.

But for a man of God, there is no safer place for his money than in the Lord's hands. I'm not just referring to the money we give, but to what we keep. Of course, in our day we have to make use of savings institutions, and we often need professionals to help us make strategic financial decisions that will enable us to leave an inheritance to our children and provide for God's work after we are gone.

You probably know Proverbs 3:5-6: "Trust in the LORD with all your heart, and lean not on your own understanding; in all your ways acknowledge Him, and He shall direct your paths." Trusting God means that we prioritize our money and all of our possessions with Him and His Kingdom in view.

That means we don't have to lie awake at night worrying about when the next dip in the stock market will come, or if we'll have enough to pay the bills. I really believe that learning to trust God is the most reasonable way to guard your money. And as we demonstrate our trust by making financial choices that honor Him and His Word, He will honor our commitment by blessing the work of our hands.

The Bible reminds us, "We brought nothing into this world, and it is certain we can carry nothing out" (1 Timothy 6:7). What a liberating truth! You and I don't have to claw our way to the top, trying to fight for every dollar we can get our hands on. We can accept what God gives us and guard it by investing in people and spreading God's Word, those things that will last forever.

## THE MONEY WE HAVE
## SHOULD BE RESPONSIBLY GIVEN

It's interesting that just after Solomon wrote Proverbs 3:5-6, he penned this verse: "Honor the LORD with your possessions, and with the firstfruits of all your increase" (v. 9). We may read verses 5-6 and pray for godly wisdom in the use of our money—and then we read an answer to our prayers!

Just as some men slice their days into seven pieces like a pie and give God one day, others cut their "money pie" into ten pieces, with one-tenth for the Lord. Now it's true that God requires the tithe, which means "one-tenth." I would have to surrender my ordination if I didn't believe that! And if you want to refresh yourself on how serious God is about the tithe, read Malachi 3:8 where He called the Israelites robbers because they withheld their tithes from Him.

### God Cares About What We Do with His Other Nine-Tenths

God bless you if you are a faithful tither to God's work. But many Christians have the math messed up here. The problem comes when we give God the tenth and say, "Okay, Lord, there's Yours. The rest is mine." Actually, the tithe was not the end of a person's giving in ancient Israel. The tithe was just the beginning of their giving, which included additional offerings of love and gratitude and praise to God. Tithing was the people's basic responsibility to God, not the limit of their generosity.

Someone may say, "But wasn't the tithe part of the Mosaic Law?" Yes, but it also preceded the Law. The tithe was in effect long before Moses, as the example of Abraham and Melchizedek shows (Genesis 14:20). Jesus also commended tithing and said it was something we ought to do (Matthew 23:23).

### Make Your Giving Generous and Systematic

It is a principle of Scripture that we should give proportionately and systematically. Many of us don't give because we don't *plan* to give. The tithe is a way we can plan our giving. The apostle Paul instructed believers, "On the first day of the week let each one of you lay something aside" (1 Corinthians 16:2). That's responsible giving.

It's easy to get hung up on the percentages here and become legalistic or slavish in our giving. Larry Burkett used to ask this question whenever a caller to his radio program wanted to know whether he should tithe on his gross or his net income: "Do you want God to bless you on the gross, or on the net?"

The truth is that we are also accountable to God for the other nine-tenths, because it is His too. Once we really grasp this, our attitude will not be how little we can give and be safe, but how much of God's money we dare keep for ourselves!

We know the Bible says, "God loves a cheerful giver" (2 Corinthians 9:7). Most pastors quote that at offering time on Sunday, but there's a lot more to it. Read the rest of that chapter and you'll see that when we are cheerful—which also implies generous—in our giving, God pours out His blessing. We can't just "name and claim" what we want from God as if He were a heavenly banker. But when our attitude is right, we can't outgive Him either!

We're to give cheerfully, not because someone squeezes us or makes an emotional appeal, or because someone has put us on a guilt trip. We give because it is the right, obedient, and blessed thing to do. Giving is not God's way to make a rich man poor. It is His way to make a poor man rich in the things that really count—and to increase our joy. God will accept the gifts of a crabby, stingy giver—but He loves a cheerful giver.

It's true that God doesn't need my money. But what I do with my money is a test of my faithfulness, and I'm going to be held accountable for my life, including my money. So much of who and what we are as men is wrapped up in what we earn. So giving is an expression of who we are, not just what we have.

But most of all, God wants to bless you. He wants you to enjoy life and the things He has given you. If they are from His hand, don't feel guilty, but use them as an act of gratitude and worship to Him. It is important to God how we get, guard, and give our money. Therefore, it ought to be important to us.

PART THREE

# A MAN OF GOD
## AND
# HIS FAMILY

# 7

# LOVING THE LADY
# IN YOUR LIFE

THERE'S A STORY THAT SAYS when God was ready to give Adam a wife, He sent an angel to talk to Adam about it. "Adam, God has noticed that you're lonely, so He is going to create a brand-new creature just for you. She's going to be called a woman."

"What is a woman?" Adam asked.

The angel said, "Well, she's someone who will be there with a smiling face when you wake up in the morning, and serve you breakfast in bed every day. She'll pick out your clothes and help you get dressed, and as you go out the door to work, she'll hug you, give you a big kiss, and think about you all day long.

"And then the moment you come in the door at night, she'll be waiting for you and plant a big kiss on your face. She'll have dinner prepared with all your favorites. And after dinner, she'll lead you to your favorite chair, put your slippers on, and maybe rub your neck or back. Then she'll sit beside you all night and be at your beck and call."

Adam replied excitedly, "Hey, I like that! How much is it going to cost me?"

"Well," the angel said, "it's expensive. Getting a woman like that is going to cost you an arm and a leg."

Adam thought for a moment and said, "What can I get for just a rib?"

That story brings a chuckle from men, but Adam got the deal of a lifetime when he got Eve that day. God gave us a rare and beautiful treasure when He gave us the gift of a woman.

There's an old saying that charity begins at home. So does being a man of God! That's why one section of this book is dedicated to helping men get their spiritual act together as husbands and fathers—although many of the principles in the next three chapters apply equally well to men who are either confirmed singles or waiting for God to bring that special lady into their lives.

All of us have women in our lives whom we need to relate to in a godly way, whether it's our wife, mother, female siblings or other relatives, or women at church and at work. Every man who wants to be a man of God has to learn how to honor, value, and cherish this special creation of God called woman.

Somebody has said if your Christianity doesn't work at home, please do the rest of us a favor and don't try to export it. I believe that if we will commit to love the lady in our life the way God tells us to love her, we will be miles down the road toward becoming true men of God.

I want to help you with the essential priority of marriage and make it very clear and simple, because the fact is that the Bible has only two basic commands to husbands in relation to how they should treat their wives. More than that, each of these commands is contained in a single verse of Scripture. And both are packed with enough truth to tell us all we need to know to build a dynamic, growing, and incredibly fulfilling marriage.

Let me give you both commands up front, so you won't be flipping to the end of the chapter to see what the second one is. They come, appropriately enough, from Peter and Paul, the two leading apostles of the church. We know for sure that Peter was married because Jesus healed his mother-in-law (Matthew 8:14-15). Many Bible scholars also believe that Paul was married at one time, and they speculate that his wife may have left him when he became a Christian. In 1 Corinthians 9:5 Paul defended his right to marry, even as Peter was married.

Here is God's command to husbands through the apostle Peter: "Husbands, likewise, dwell with them [your wives] with understanding, giving honor to the wife, as to the weaker vessel, and as being heirs together of the grace of life, that your prayers may not be hindered" (1 Peter 3:7). And then from Paul comes this word: "Husbands, love your wives, just as Christ also loved the church and gave Himself for her" (Ephesians 5:25). Both of these verses are loaded with meaning.

## LIVE WITH YOUR LADY IN AN UNDERSTANDING WAY

The context of 1 Peter 3:7 is especially important. Verses 1-6 are a beautiful description of the responsive nature of a woman and the influence she can have in her home. The emphasis in these verses is the way that a godly woman responds to and pleases God by her response to her husband, even if he is an unbeliever.

A wife is commanded here to be submissive to her husband, as is also the case in Ephesians 5:22. But in neither place is a husband allowed to take advantage of his wife's submissive and responsive spirit. On the contrary, we husbands are to guard that precious gift and cherish the woman who gives it to us.

This is why Peter began his exhortation to husbands in verse 7 with the word "likewise." In other words, just as godly women like Sarah obeyed and pleased God, husbands can obey and please Him by treating their wives with "understanding," or literally, with "intelligence."

Have you ever done something and immediately said to yourself angrily, "Why did I do that? That wasn't smart!" We all do things against our better judgment, and sometimes I'm afraid that men just aren't smart in the way they relate to their wives. If we really stop and think about it, most of us know how our wives like to be treated and what they need from us. And most of us know what irritates and frustrates the lady God gave us. We just don't always take the time it requires to live intelligently with our wives.

But there's more to this idea of living intelligently with our wives than not saying or doing things that upset them. It also has to do with observing and studying our wives so that we know them well. Now it's true that women are far better equipped than men for the difficult work of interpersonal relationships. But that doesn't let men off the hook. It just means we have to work harder at it.

Now I admit my frailties at this point. After thirty years of studying women, a well-known psychologist said, "I really don't know what it is they want." And many of us men would have to say the same thing. But the admonition and challenge to us in Scripture is to study our wives, to pay such close attention to them that we can love them the way they need to be loved.

## Women Want and Need Togetherness

One area where a husband can show some "smarts" in relation to his wife is by realizing that she needs and wants togetherness. Loneliness in marriage is being called the virus of this generation, and it's usually the wife who feels it. I'm not talking about just being in the same house with your wife, or taking her along on the fishing trip. Togetherness is as much emotional and spiritual as it is physical.

The problem is that men tend to view courtship and marriage as a challenge and a conquest. They're very considerate and attentive and affectionate while they're winning the girl, but once she's won and the chase is over, they tend to put their wife on the shelf like a trophy and head off to conquer new challenges and climb new mountains.

Meanwhile, the wife is left alone, wondering what happened to the man who showed her so much attention and love and affection. When the Bible says to "dwell with" our wives, there is more in view than being under the same roof.

## Women Want and Need Tenderness

Living with the lady in your life in an understanding or intelligent way also involves giving her honor, or cherishing her with tenderness and affection. Peter called the wife a "weaker vessel," but this term in no sense implies any inferiority on the woman's part.

A woman is weaker in the sense that fine china is more delicate than the ordinary dishes you would use every day. A woman is of equal value with a man, for Peter said later that the two are "heirs together of the grace of life."

I could give you pages of examples of ways in which a woman is built differently than a man and is not as physically strong in terms of sheer brute strength. But in terms of vitality, many times women can outwork men. And it's a well-known fact that women in this country outlive men on average by three to four years.

A woman is also very different from a man psychologically and emotionally. People love to write songs about a woman's tenderness and need for care and attention, but judging by the way many husbands treat their wives, you'd never know they ever listened to a radio or owned a CD player.

Here is some guys' idea of showing tenderness: "Listen, Dear, after you finish the dishes and ironing and get the kids to bed, how about making me a sandwich and then come sit down for a while?"

### Women Want and Need Empathy

Comments like this won't exactly win you a sensitivity award! What they do is reveal an insensitivity to the way women are made. Empathy is a good word for this because it means "to feel with." There are legions of wives who could say, "My husband doesn't really know or understand me at all." One reason is that it takes time and effort to know another person, and not many men are willing to spend that kind of time.

On one episode of a popular television sitcom, the husband and leading character put his hands to his head and started writhing around in agony when his wife said they needed to talk. "Oh, no!" he moaned, emphasizing his words. "Do we have to *talk?* Please tell me we don't have to *talk!*"

Sorry, pal, but if you're married, you have to talk sometimes.

Women are more personal and social beings than men. They are much more attuned to people and even to the environment around them than men. That's why a husband and wife might come home from a party or some other social event, and the wife will say, "Wow! Can you believe what was happening in that room tonight? The tension was so thick you could have cut it with a knife."

At this point, the husband is wondering if he was at the same party as his wife, because he didn't notice anything. But his wife picked up on a look, a gesture, or a word that not only told her something was going on, but who was involved and what the issue was. It's amazing.

Now you may ask, "Jack, does empathizing with my wife mean I have to learn all the stuff she knows and become as good as she is about reading and relating to people?"

I hope not, brother, or we're all in trouble. We'll never be as good as our wives at being a woman, and thank the Lord we don't have to be. One man said the nice thing about being a guy is that you can visit people without having to bring a small gift, and you can go to the bathroom alone.

I don't understand why women go to the bathroom in groups. I've never been sitting around a table with guys and said, "Hey Steve, you want to go to the bathroom?" I can't figure that one out, but I think it has something to do with relationships. It gives women an opportunity to empathize with each other.

## Women Want and Need Spiritual Encouragement

You ought to be thankful as a husband that the lady in your life has a huge capacity to relate to God and to others. Many women are great examples and inspirations to their husbands in this regard, but too many times a wife does not get the spiritual encouragement and sharing of the things of God that she needs in return.

Jesus said the two greatest commandments are to love God with all your heart and to love your neighbor as yourself (Matthew 22:37-39). Women are able to obey these commands in a way that it often takes men years to learn. If a husband is the head of the home, and I believe he should be, then his wife is the heart of the home.

My experience as a pastor has been that many Christian men feel they need to be spiritual giants themselves before they can have any spiritual input with their wives. But that simply isn't true. A lot of women will tell you, "I don't expect my husband to be the apostle Paul. I just wish he would pray with me once in a while, or read the Bible with me."

There are women who have been married for years who say that their husbands have never prayed with them. That's at the opposite end of the spectrum from living with the lady in your life in an understanding and intelligent way.

## Women Want and Need Appreciation

God made your lady with a desire and a need to be appreciated and noticed, to know that you're paying attention to her. We've already said that one of the most hurtful things a man can do to his wife is to push her aside and exclude her from his life. There are plenty of married men who want to do their own thing, which does not include their wives.

I often tell young couples that the best definition of marriage is two givers who are trying to out-give each other. If you start giving of yourself to your wife, you will be amazed at how much she will out-give you. God created a woman with a wonderful capacity to respond to the love, appreciation, and attention of her man.

## Women Want and Need Time

You knew I was going to get to this one. It's impossible to live with your lady in a sensitive and intelligent way without investing huge amounts of time in your marriage.

How do you spend your time away from your work? We all have responsibilities, and you may not have much discretionary income in your budget, but all of us have discretionary time. Some homes today should have revolving doors as the people who live there fly in and fly out. One teenager defined home as "the place where you wait while someone else is using the car."

Studies show that the average married couple spends about thirty-seven minutes a day in conversation, and that may be stretching it for some couples. That also doesn't say how many of those minutes are spent in small talk and coordinating the day's events.

Yet the very nature of marriage calls for unhurried time to talk and listen to each other, to look in your lady's eyes and give her your undivided attention. If you haven't done that in a while, start slowly: It may scare your wife if you suddenly look into her eyes and really listen!

It's very instructive that the biblical term for the sexual act of marriage is to "know" each other. That suggests a process that comes long before the act of sexual expression itself. Christian psychologist Kevin Leman wrote a book titled *Sex Begins in the Kitchen*. Men often try to rush relationships, but women understand far better than we do that any relationship worth developing takes time.

When a man says to his lady by his words and actions, "I want to spend time with you," she will feel special. Whether you take your wife out on a weekly date, a walk, or a get-away adventure, build time into your life for your wife.

### Women Want and Need Conversation

We don't need scientific studies to tell us that on the whole, women are more verbal than men. A lot of guys would say, "Hey, one thing at a time. I'm still working on listening." That's great, but your lady also wants you to talk to her. One of the challenges of communication in marriage is that men and women communicate on an entirely different level. A woman may say she has a problem she wants to talk about, and the man is thinking, *Okay, let's get this out here so I can figure out how to fix it and get back to my game.*

But a quick solution is seldom what a woman wants. She wants to talk it through and see how her husband feels about the situation and her feelings and response to it.

It's also common for a wife to want to know more about her husband's work, or a trip he made or meeting he attended—not in terms of the deals made, but who was there and what they talked about and how he felt about the way things went.

This isn't always easy for men, because we often don't remember who was there or other personal details that are of interest to our wives. One guy said, "My wife asked me how I felt about what so-and-so said. I didn't know I was supposed to feel anything about it until she asked me."

That's okay, brother. Just hang in there and keep talking and listening to your lady.

### Women Want and Need Praise

Praise is powerful. Praise releases the power and presence of God. So why shouldn't a genuine, heartfelt word of praise release the power in your marriage?

When we praise God, we adore Him for who He is and what He has done. We have to know God to praise Him, and the same is true of our wives. Our wives deserve our praise and blessing for being the kind of godly women they are as a wife and mother. One of the encouraging developments in the church over the past few decades is the number of Christian men who are learning how to praise God and are entering into it enthusiastically. Let's carry that home and let our wives know we are blown away by the incredible lady God has given us. If you don't know where to start, try thanking God for your wife and telling Him what she means to you—in her presence. Tell *God* how much you cherish her, and it will be easier to start telling her regularly.

### Women Want and Need Consideration

The lady in your life also deserves your consideration and respect. One wife said her husband used to scramble around and open the door for her when they were dating. Now she says she barely gets her foot inside the car door before he roars off.

That's not just laziness on her husband's part, although it is that.

It's a lack of respect and consideration. It doesn't always take a whole lot of thoughtfulness to make women feel special. Let me give you a good biblical reason to respect your wife. She is your equal, your sister in Christ. You are "heirs together of the grace of life."

## You Want and Need Your Prayers Answered

Peter gave husbands a "bottom line" at the end of 1 Peter 3:7. One reason we are to live with our wives in an understanding way is that "[our] prayers may not be hindered." God is so serious about this business of our love and consideration for our wives that if we're messing up here, our prayers are bouncing off the ceiling.

I picture God the Father with His hand up—like our parents did when we were in the wrong and tried to justify ourselves or ask for something—saying, "I don't want to hear from you until you're ready to make that wrong right."

Some men wonder why they can never seem to get their act together spiritually. The answer may be sitting across the breakfast table from them. I don't want God hindering my prayers, because that means I'm dead in the water. Let's make sure we are treating our lady with sensitivity and respect.

## Love Your Lady in a Self-Sacrificing Way

Learning to understand and live with his wife in the way Peter described is a tall assignment for any man. One guy's response to this was to ask, "Who could ever understand a woman?" I don't have the definitive answer to that, but part of the fun and the challenge of marriage is getting to know that wonderful lady God has brought into your life.

There's a second challenge we need to put alongside this first one. The two are related but also have their distinctive elements. The Bible tells us, "Husbands, love your wives, just as Christ also loved the church and gave Himself up for her" (Ephesians 5:25). Since Christ's love for the church is the greatest example of love in the universe, loving our wives as Christ intended is the greatest challenge we have in life.

It's important to understand why Paul used Jesus' love for His church as the basis for a husband's love for his wife. The question is how Jesus loved the church, and we're going to look at that. I also want you to see that Christ relates to His church on the basis of a covenant, not just a contract.

We're beginning to hear more these days about the covenant of marriage, and that's good. A covenant is a solemn promise that is meant to be kept and not broken. Human contracts are broken all the time, although that's not the way it should be. Many contracts even allow for a way out if one party or the other doesn't fulfill the contract's conditions.

But a covenant is something different altogether. It is a binding agreement, a promise, a vow of faithfulness. In the Old Testament, the word often used to describe the making of a covenant was the verb "to cut." You can see this clearly in Genesis 15, when God "cut" a covenant with Abraham. The covenant was sealed with the blood of an animal that was killed. This sacrifice solemnized the covenant ceremony and symbolized the permanence of the covenant.

God has made an unconditional covenant of salvation with us in Christ. The Greek word "testament" is literally "covenant," and we live under the new covenant that has been ratified and sealed with the blood of Christ. Nothing can break this covenant, and God will never go back on it. We can praise Him for that!

In the same way, God intended the marriage relationship to be an unconditional, lifelong promise of love and faithfulness between a man and a woman. A marriage is a divine covenant, a divine transaction. That's why preachers remind the bride and groom that when they proclaim their love and loyalty until they are separated by death, they are making their vows before God as well as the witnesses looking on.

Every marriage, yours and mine included, will face challenges and difficulties. As men of God, we must make sure that we are doing our part to see that our marriages don't just survive, but thrive.

Wives are commanded in Ephesians 5:22 to submit to their husbands as unto Christ. That's a real challenge, because most husbands have a long way to go to be like Christ. But I believe the bulk of the responsibility for a Christ-centered marriage is squarely on the shoulders of men—and our calling is clear! Our love for our wives is to be as pure, unconditional, sacrificial, and sanctifying as Christ's love for the church. Do you think we need some help with that? So do I!

That's why I want to look deeper into Ephesians 5 and try to identify the ways that Christ loves us as His people, so that we as husbands can begin to get a handle on how we should love our wives. Jesus does not coerce or pressure us to love Him or submit to Him. He calls us to respond to His love from our hearts. Love that is forced and bullied is not love.

And by the way, let me make an observation before we go any further. The Bible does *not* say, "Husbands, make your wives submit to you as to the Lord," although I'm afraid that's how too many men read it. Our wives' submission is a spiritual issue between them and the Lord. We are called to love them with a love so Christlike that they will naturally respond to our leadership. That brings us back to the question, how does Christ love the church, and how are we to love our wives?

### We Must Love Our Wives Selflessly

The first thing Paul said about Jesus and His love for the church is that He "gave Himself" for the church. This is selfless love, the same kind of love I am to show to my wife.

The biggest problem in most marriages is selfishness—adults acting like children, insisting on having their own way. A person who has not learned to yield to God's authority in his life is a poor candidate for "husbandhood." As long as we are demanding what we want, we don't have time to care about what our wives need or want.

We need a new attitude in our marriages—the attitude of humility that Jesus exhibited when He laid aside the robes of glory to take on human flesh. Paul's magnificent plea for humility based on Christ's example (Philippians 2:1-8) should be required reading for husbands about once a week.

In fact, I seriously encourage you to memorize this passage in Philippians and make it a part of your daily determination to follow Christ as His disciple and love your wife with His love. Marriage is a wonderful training ground for a man who truly wants to be a man of God in every area of his life.

The first thing that has to happen if the covenant of marriage is to be kept as God intended is that there must be a death to self. Somebody said, "Every marriage needs one wedding and two funerals." The wedding brings together two lives, but the death of self in both the husband and the wife allows them to live as one flesh and one spirit. There are two kinds of husbands in a marriage, the givers and the takers. Which kind of husband are you?

I often tell young couples that if they go into marriage for what they can get out of it, they will most likely be disappointed. If you marry a woman for what she can give you and the way she can build you up and enhance you, you're on the wrong track. But if your desire is to find out what you can give to your wife and how you can pour yourself out in loving and serving her, you are on your way to a great marriage.

### We Must Love Our Wives Sacrificially

When the Bible says Jesus gave Himself for the church, it's talking about His death. The ultimate act of sacrifice was when Jesus allowed Himself to be stretched out and nailed to the cross to demonstrate His love for us (Romans 5:8).

Some husbands hear this and say, "Well, I'd be willing to die for my wife if it came to that. That would be the easy part. It's living with her that's killing me."

I really believe that most of us would do whatever it takes to defend our wives if they were in mortal danger. But the real self-sacrifice we are called upon to make is to die every day to our own desires and preferences and opinions in order to love our wives and give ourselves to them sacrificially. It's this kind of daily sacrifice that is so hard for men to make.

That's why it is so crucial to understand that marriage is a covenant in which two people bind themselves together in love for life. It takes the love of Jesus Christ to hold a marriage together, because His love is very different than human love.

There are three Greek words for love used in the Bible. One is *eros*, the base of the word *erotic*. This is physical or sexual love, which is very important in a marriage. God gave the gift of sex between a man and a woman within the covenant of marriage so that they could express their love and enjoy deep intimacy.

A second biblical word for love is *phileo*, commonly referred to as "brotherly love." This is the love of friends, the warmth and caring experienced by people who truly like each other and connect at a deep personal level.

I want you to know that I don't just love my wife, Deb, with all my heart. I also like her a lot! We're best friends. She's the person I'd rather be with more than anyone else on earth. It's amazing how many married couples don't really seem to like each other. They appear to live completely separate lives, take separate vacations, and the whole bit. My question is, why would you marry someone you don't like, and like a lot? If I could answer that for everyone, I'd be rich.

You can build *phileo* love with your wife the same way you develop a close friendship—by spending time together, by talking with each other, by resolving conflicts when they occur, by doing things together that you enjoy, and by finding out what makes the other person happy. It has been said that you can divorce a wife, but you can't divorce your best friend.

The third word for love in Scripture is the familiar and wonderful word *agape*, which is the word used in Ephesians 5:25 for a husband's love and for Christ's self-sacrificing love.

*Agape* is what put Christ on the cross. As *eros* is the physical side of love and *phileo* is the emotional side, *agape* is the spiritual side of love. It is the sacrificial love of Christ for His church, and the sacrificial love a husband is called to show to his wife.

## We Must Love Our Wives Sanctifyingly

Paul's instruction to husbands in Ephesians 5 continues in verses 26 and 27, where we read that Christ gave Himself for the church "that He might sanctify and cleanse her with the washing of water by the word, that He might present her to Himself a glorious church, not having spot or wrinkle or any such thing, but that she should be holy and without blemish."

I have flaws, blemishes, and sinful spots in my life, and Jesus cleanses me from all sin. He sanctifies me, which means to "make holy." Jesus is my Sanctifier as well as my Savior.

Did you know that a husband is to be the sanctifier of his wife? Not in the sense of salvation, for only Jesus can do that. But our love for our wives should be a purifying and uplifting love that brings a holy presence into our marriage.

As men of God, we are to be both prophets and priests in our homes. We have a spiritual responsibility to pray for our wives and protect them spiritually, and to teach the Word of God to our families. The husband, not the wife, is to be the spiritual leader of the home.

This scares a lot of men because they either don't feel adequate to lead their wives into a deeper experience of God and His holiness, or they really don't have any strong desire to do so. Too many men let their wives handle the spiritual side of the home. "Oh, you know, I let the little lady take care of that. She's more spiritual than I am, and she's a lot better at teaching the kids."

Well, if your wife is a spiritually mature woman and loves to teach your children the things of God, you are blessed. But that doesn't relieve you of your responsibility to take the spiritual lead in your marriage and family. That doesn't mean you have to do it all yourself or sit the family down while Dad lectures. But it does mean that you need to be a growing Christian who has a sanctifying presence in your home.

Christ's goal is to present the church as His spotless and pure bride before God. If we are to love our wives with the same sanctifying love, then our goal should be to present to God a radiant Christian wife.

Abraham Lincoln once interviewed a man seeking a position in his administration, but he turned the candidate down. When asked why by an aide, Lincoln said, "I didn't like his face."

"What do you mean by that?" the aide asked.

"Every man over forty is responsible for his face," the president replied. Lincoln was talking about the man's countenance and what it revealed about him.

I'd like to paraphrase what Lincoln said and say that every man who has been married for any length of time is responsible for his wife's face. You can often tell what kind of spiritual influence a man is at home just by looking into his wife's face.

If you see anger, fear, resentment, or sorrow reflected in a wife's countenance, you can be pretty sure her husband is not leading and loving her God's way. But when you see a woman whose face glows with the radiance and joy of Christ, it's a safe guess that her husband is getting the job done at home.

Let me remind you, brother, that your first job is not at work or at church, but at home. We're to love our wives with a purifying, sanctifying love, to help them grow in the grace and knowledge of Jesus Christ (2 Peter 3:18).

### We Must Love Our Wives Satisfyingly

Here's a fourth way we are to love our wives. Paul wrote, "So husbands ought to love their own wives as their own bodies; he who loves his wife loves himself" (Ephesians 5:28).

Every man loves his own body and tries to satisfy its needs. If you're thirsty, you get a drink; if you're hungry, you get something to eat; if you're tired, you get some sleep; if you itch, you scratch. In the same way we are to love our wives, because in marriage a man and a woman become one flesh.

Would you like to know the secret to a happy marriage? Here it is. This is worth the price of the book. If you want a happy marriage, quit trying to be happy and start trying to make your wife happy. When you satisfy your wife and give her joy and pleasure by the way you love her, you will find satisfaction you never thought possible because, remember, your wife is designed to be a responder. You can be good to yourself by being good to your wife.

The amazing thing is how little it often takes to make our wives happy. I'm not saying you should seek to do as little as possible, just that there are so many little things a husband can do to satisfy his wife's desire for his attention, affection, and affirmation. One wife said, "I'm sure my husband would jump in a fire for me. I just wish he would go for a walk with me sometime. That would be so enjoyable for me."

The Bible says that Jesus endured the cross "for the joy that was set before Him" (Hebrews 12:2). Jesus experienced the deepest joy that anyone can ever know, the joy of giving yourself for someone you love. And the best part is that when you give yourself to your wife to satisfy her, the love and joy come back to you in abundance.

Too many men think of their wives as a possession to enjoy, like a new car, rather than as a person to experience. The problem with our cars is that when they get older, the tendency is to want to discard them for a newer, shinier model.

But your wife is not a car to trade in when the newness wears off! She is a magnificent creation of God, the greatest gift He could give you this side of heaven. The best investment you can make in your own happiness and sense of satisfaction in life is to invest your life in loving your lady satisfyingly.

## We Must Love Our Wives Supremely

Again, in Ephesians 5 we find this incredible statement: "For this reason a man shall leave his father and mother and be joined to his wife, and the two shall become one flesh" (v. 31).

In the New King James Version of the Bible, this verse is in italics because it is a quote from Genesis 2:24, the very words of God Himself as He performed the first marriage, between Adam and Eve.

Why is a man to leave his father and mother in favor of his

wife? Because the marriage relationship is supreme over all other earthly relationships. The problem in too many marriages is men and women who are trying to cleave to each other without cutting the apron strings. Your love for your wife has to be supreme and preeminent over all other ties.

A man went to see his pastor with a worried look on his face. When the pastor asked what was wrong, the man said, "Pastor, I'm worried that I love my wife more than I should."

The pastor looked at the man for a minute and realized he was serious. So this wise man of God said, "Well, let me ask you. Do you love your wife as much as Jesus loves the church?"

The man looked down and said, "Well, no, I can't say that."

"Then get with it, brother!" the pastor replied.

## We Must Love Our Wives Steadfastly

"The two shall become one flesh" (Ephesians 5:31b) is the crowning declaration and wonderful mystery of what it means for two people to be joined in marriage. Jesus said concerning marriage, "What God has joined together, let not man separate" (Matthew 19:6). You can't separate one flesh without doing great damage or even causing death.

Sometimes a man will say, "I want a divorce because I just don't love my wife anymore." It's easy to quit on a marriage, but it takes godly commitment to be steadfast in your love. Of course, marriage is not always easy. It wasn't easy for God to save you from your sins and the hell those sins deserved. But aren't you glad Jesus didn't quit on you halfway to Calvary?

And aren't you glad God doesn't quit on you every time you mess up and do something wrong? Your salvation is forever because you are being held in God's hands, and no one can "snatch" you out of His hand (John 10:29). Nothing can separate you from God's love in Christ Jesus (Romans 8:35-39). We are bone of His bone and flesh of His flesh.

This is the same commitment God wants us to make toward our marriages. I have become a part of Deb, and she is a part of me. Divorce is so destructive and damaging because it is not just separating two people; it is an amputation. It is the separation of two lives that have been bound together and blessed together in Jesus Christ.

Therefore, we are to love our wives steadfastly. Persevere through any pain or pressure, but do not quit on your promise to your wife! Honor God by honoring your wife.

You say, "How am I going to do that? I'm not Jesus."

I remind you that Jesus lives in you by the Holy Spirit—and as you allow the Spirit to fill you day by day, you can be filled with the love of Jesus for your wife every day of your life.

# 8

# PROTECTING AND BLESSING YOUR FAMILY

MY FRIEND DR. DAVID JEREMIAH tells the story of a young father who took his two small children to see their mother, who was working at the hospital on Mother's Day. The family gave their gifts to Mom and then left, the father carrying his three-month-old son in an infant car seat while big sister toddled alongside.

They went down to the parking garage, which was dark as these garages often are. Dad gently set his son on the roof of the car while he went to the other side and buckled his daughter into her seat. But in the process the father forgot that his son was still on the roof of the car. Dad got in, started the car, and drove off with his infant son riding on the roof.

Unbelievably, the father not only drove out into traffic, but merged onto the interstate. No one around him seemed to notice the infant on top of the car, or if they did no one honked or tried to stop the car. It wasn't until the car was at freeway speed that this father heard a screeching noise. He turned around to look at his son and suddenly realized he wasn't safely buckled in the back seat. That's when Dad looked in the rearview mirror and, to his horror, saw his baby sliding off the back of the car and into the oncoming traffic.

What happened next is even more unbelievable. A man who was driving behind this father saw the baby's car seat fly off the car and into the road. At first he thought it was just some trash that someone had run over, and then he thought it was a doll. But he looked again and realized it was a baby.

So this man slammed on his brakes and turned his car into the middle lanes of traffic to stop the other cars. He jumped out of his car, ran to the child, picked up that little baby alive and healthy, and placed him in his father's arms.

I believe this story is in many ways a picture of the world our families and children are facing today. They are sitting in the road, as it were, with traffic rushing toward them and spiritual danger on every side, but lacking real protection. And the truly unfortunate thing is that Dad, who is called to be the family's spiritual protector, often doesn't realize the danger until he looks backward in the rearview mirror after the family has already crashed.

No one ever said that being a father is easy, but I am absolutely convinced that a dad who commits himself to lead his wife and children according to the principles of God's Word can be successful. In fact, the Bible gives us the best manual on fatherhood— and on life in general—ever written: the book of Proverbs. Many people think of Proverbs as just a string of pithy sayings, but it is so much more than that.

Proverbs is rightly included in the Wisdom books of the Bible. It is filled with godly wisdom, much of it written from a father to his child. The book of Proverbs is Holy Spirit–inspired wisdom for raising our children. Its principles don't always jibe with pop psychology, or even much of what we are hearing in Christian circles today.

But Proverbs is tough, straight-on, and at times gut-wrenching counsel as to how we're to live our lives and lead our families. It deals forthrightly with subjects every father will face with his children, from money to sex to education to friends to emotions and a lot more. Proverbs teaches us how to make a life, and not just a living. The subject of this immensely practical portion of the Word of God is skillful living.

That's why I have taken several slices of wisdom from the

Proverbs—to help you and me as fathers in the all-important task of protecting our children from spiritual danger as we seek to raise them in the Lord, blessing them with our own example and encouragement, and the truth of God's Word. The principles I want to share with you are straight from the Scripture, and I believe if you will take them to heart and put them into practice you will be able to teach your children God's way.

## TEACH YOUR CHILDREN TO FEAR AND LOVE GOD

In Proverbs 1:7 we read these familiar words: "The fear of the LORD is the beginning of knowledge." The fear of the Lord is one of the constant themes of Proverbs, because this is where wise living begins. This is not a cringing fear that causes a person to quake in God's presence or to run from Him. Godly fear is recognizing God's holiness, greatness, and awesomeness, and responding with adoration and deep respect for Him.

As Christian fathers, we want our children to love God—but biblically, to love God is to fear Him. They are two sides of the same coin. That's why I put fear ahead of love in the title of this section. Someone has described the fear of the Lord as love on its knees.

You would have a hard time believing your son if he said, "Dad, I love you," but totally disrespected you and disregarded your counsel at every turn. Teaching our children to love and fear God will give them a healthy respect for God and His Word, a healthy desire to obey Him, and a healthy fear of the consequences of sin and rebellion in their lives. The Scripture says, "Do not be deceived, God is not mocked; for whatever a man sows, that he will also reap" (Galatians 6:7).

Children must be taught to fear and love God because there is a streak of rebellion, a propensity to sin, born in the heart of every child. Our children get it from us, and we are the ones who have to deal with it while we have the chance to mold and shape them.

"Foolishness is bound up in the heart of a child" (Proverbs 22:15). The psalmist said of the wicked, "They go astray as soon as they are born, speaking lies" (Psalm 58:3). You don't have to teach a child to lie. It comes naturally, just as it does to us. It seems to me that fathers don't have as much trouble as mothers believing their little angels are capable of sin. Maybe that's because little boys are usually more devilish than little girls, and we can remember what we were like. But whatever the case, any child left completely to himself will pursue a course of sin and rebellion against God. So teach your children to fear and love God from their earliest days.

I love Proverbs 14:26-27, where we read, "In the fear of the LORD there is strong confidence, and His children will have a place of refuge. The fear of the LORD is a fountain of life, to turn one away from the snares of death."

## TEACH YOUR CHILDREN TO GUARD THEIR MINDS

The Bible says we are not what we think we are, but we *are* what we think. "As [a person] thinks in his heart, so is he" (Proverbs 23:7). This is why Solomon advised us, "Keep [or guard] your heart with all diligence, for out of it spring the issues of life" (Proverbs 4:23).

Of course, the "heart" refers to the inner person and the inner life. We need to teach our children to protect themselves against the influences that would corrupt their minds and lead them away from Christ.

It's amazing how relevant the Bible is. There is a verse you may have heard many times that takes on a whole new meaning in this age of the Internet: "I will set nothing wicked before my eyes" (Psalm 101:3).

Think about this verse in terms of the ability that we and our children have to set an endless array of images before our eyes right there on our computers. Now I don't want to talk about Internet pornography again, except to say that it is our responsibility as fathers not only to protect our children from the stuff that is out there, but to set the highest standards for them by our own actions.

Our children are exposed to things today that many of our grandparents never learned about. I heard of one dad who told his son he wanted to have a talk with him about the birds and the bees, and the boy said, "Sure, Dad. What is it you want to know?"

By the time children today reach the teenage years, they've seen it all and heard it all. And some of them have done it all, because we as parents haven't always done our job of protecting their minds.

Child development experts are talking about the vanishing childhood of the American child. Kids are growing up faster than ever before, and that's not all good. In fact, most of it is not good at all. The moral and mental environment in America is toxic to our children.

We can't always keep our children from some things that are base and vile and ugly. We can't put them in a monastery somewhere, and even if we could, it wouldn't do any good in terms of keeping their minds and hearts pure. God does not expect us to isolate our children, but to insulate them from the world and its ways by teaching them to be wise, to have biblical "smarts" so they discern between the true and the false.

The best way to protect your child's mind is to fill it with God's Word. Experts in detecting counterfeit money spend the vast majority of their time examining real currency. The best way to spot a fake is to know what the real looks like.

We can also expose our children to godly influences. This is where your involvement in a Christ-exalting, Bible-believing, Spirit-filled church can have a powerful impact on your family. When your family is under the teaching and modeling of God's Word, other people who also love Christ and want the best for your kids have the opportunity for positive input in their lives. And if you're the father of a teenager, you know that a teen will often take instruction and even correction from a youth leader or coach better than from you.

The goal is to build character into your children. Character is one of those concepts that sounds hard to attain, but a person's character is nothing more than the sum total of his thought life. Since the Bible says you are what you think, we fathers had better make sure our children are being fed—notice I didn't say force-fed—a steady diet of God's truth.

And guess what, Dad? If you are feeding on the Word and so hungry for it that it means more to you than your daily food (check out Job 23:12), your kids will want a taste of the good stuff you're enjoying.

## TEACH YOUR CHILDREN TO CHOOSE THEIR FRIENDS WISELY

This is a recurring theme in the Proverbs. One verse pretty well sums it up: "He who walks with wise men will be wise, but the companion of fools will be destroyed" (Proverbs 13:20).

Show me the people you hang out with, and I'll show you the kind of person you are or will become. And what is true for me and for you is true for our children.

One of the problems here is the same problem we talked about above. Our children are imperfect, with a bent toward sin, and so, left to themselves, they may be drawn to unsavory companions because they often can't see the pitfalls we can see.

A boy was asked one day if he was a good little boy. In a burst of complete honesty, he said, "No, actually I'm not. I'm the kind of boy my mommy doesn't want me playing with."

Reminds me of the great line by the late comedian Groucho Marx: "I wouldn't join any club that would have me as a member."

One of the challenges of being a parent is that parenting happens at the busiest time of our lives. Some grandparents say, "I could have been a much better parent if I had had the time that I have now."

And because we are so busy, we sometimes turn our children over to others to raise. Especially when their children reach the teenage years, some dads just throw up their hands and say, "They've got their own friends, and I can't do anything about it." But that's a give-up attitude that won't help anything.

If your children are teens, it's true that they will choose their own friends. But you can still get to know those friends and what kind of families they come from. And let me give you a word of encouragement. Even though your teen may think dear old Dad is a poster child for being out of it, a teen's friends often think their friends' parents are cool, especially if you have an open door and a listening ear, and there's plenty of food. Don't allow your kids to seal themselves off in their own world.

And if your children are younger, give them strong guidance in terms of helping them choose good friends.

The Bible says, "Evil company corrupts good habits" (1 Corinthians 15:33). It's a fact of life that some kids are just trouble waiting to happen—and your child doesn't need to be hanging out with trouble. Here's an exercise that will bless you and return incredible dividends in your children's lives. Read through the Proverbs with a pencil and paper, and mark down passages that talk about the importance of choosing good companions and avoiding evil ones (Proverbs 1:8-19 and 2:10-15 are two good starters). Then share these passages with your children, and talk about them over dinner.

And by the way, teach your children that they will have to stand alone sometimes for the truth. Teach your children about the power of one person standing for God, as the teenager Daniel did in Babylon.

## SET A GODLY EXAMPLE FOR YOUR CHILDREN

"I have taught you in the way of wisdom; I have led you in right paths" (Proverbs 4:11).

Do you see it? We can't lead our children where we haven't been ourselves. God cannot do something through us until He does something in and to us! We need to set a godly example, because we know that whether for good or ill, our children are mostly going to turn out like us.

That's a pretty scary thought, isn't it? Well, let's remember that our kids don't expect us to be perfect, but they do have a right to expect us to be real. You're going to make mistakes as a dad. We all do. When you do, apologize to your children and move forward. Children are very forgiving if they know you are sincerely trying to do your best. They just want to see the real deal in Dad's life.

Again, the point is not to be perfect. The point is to be consistent in your walk with Christ. I like to paraphrase Proverbs 20:7 by saying, "If you live right and honestly, your children will be blessed."

I would rather die than disappoint my family or be a stumbling block to my wife or children in their walk with Christ. Above all else, I want my children to know that their dad loves God and serves Him. Deb and I determined early on in our marriage that we would guard against trying to fake it in the ministry or in our home. And we also decided that our home was going to be a fun and positive and exciting place.

I've given you a lot of serious and sobering things to consider, but I also want to say, have fun being a dad! Learn to laugh with your kids and at yourself, and they'll listen better to you when you're serious.

You say, "I think it may be too late for me. How can I change my child at this stage?" Well, there are no easy answers to that, but I would say begin by asking God to change you, and then watch God change your child.

## GIVE YOUR CHILDREN
## UNCONDITIONALLY TO CHRIST

Our children have their whole lives ahead of them to serve and bring glory to Christ. If we want their lives to count for Christ, let's give them to Him early without anything held back.

One day the great evangelist D. L. Moody was asked, "Well, how many conversions did you have last night in your crusade?"

He said, "Two and a half!"

"Oh," the person said. "You mean two adults and a child."

"No," Moody replied, "two children and one adult." Moody understood that children have a full life to live for Christ, while an adult who gets saved has only half a life left.

There has been a big emphasis on keeping ourselves and our children safe since 9/11. There was a bomb threat one day at a high school near our church, and hundreds of students were brought to the church for their safety.

Many of those families attend our church, and I said to my wife, Deb, "What should I say to these parents?"

She said, "Tell them we can't always keep our children safe. We can't control or fix every situation for them."

There is only one safe place on earth for us and our children, and that is in the center of God's will. A. W. Tozer, the great Christian writer of another era, said, "Everything in life which we commit to God is really safe. And everything which we refuse to commit to Him is never safe."

Our children are a gift from God. They are on loan to us for a very few years. At the very beginning of your children's lives, offer them to God, and then spend every day working to make sure they follow Jesus Christ.

I have a friend who sent his college-age daughter to Mexico for a semester of missions service. People asked him if he was afraid for her safety, but he and his wife had already worked through that issue. His standard answer to that question was, "My daughter is going in the will of God, which means she'll be as safe in Mexico as she would be in her own bedroom upstairs."

## GIVE YOUR CHILDREN YOUR BLESSING

Authors Gary Smalley and John Trent did the church a huge service several years ago when they wrote their book, *The Blessing*. It awakened many fathers to their need to make sure they pass on a Christian heritage to their children by giving them their blessing.

The concept of a father blessing his children is as old as the book of Genesis. Isaac called in his son Esau to give him his blessing, although it was stolen by Jacob (Genesis 27). Later Jacob himself, just before his death, pronounced a blessing on his sons (Genesis 49).

This is more than just saying to your child, "God bless you."

Blessing your child involves knowing them well enough to see the gifts and abilities God has given them, helping your kids see their gifts, and encouraging them to use those gifts to the glory of God.

There are probably legions of grown men in our world who would give anything if their fathers had said to them, "Son, I want you to know that you don't have to do or be anything other than what you are to make me proud of you. And you have my blessing and support in following God's call on your life."

Blessing your children is not a one-time event, but a process of building their confidence that they can be successful in the will of God for their lives. Kids need a cheerleader, and Dad can fill that role. I thank the Lord for my dad, Tom Graham, who supported me every step of the way in my growing-up years. He was always there. He blessed his two sons, and we are both preaching the gospel today.

## COVER YOUR CHILDREN WITH PRAYER

I can't think of any more important lesson in life than to know how to pray for your children. I want to help you do that as we cap off this chapter with a biblical strategy you can use to pray for your kids.

We're in spiritual warfare for our children and families, and prayer is the most important weapon we can use. In Ephesians 6:10-17, the apostle Paul spoke of this battle and the weapons God has given us to defeat the enemy. As we take up these weapons, we need to be "praying always with all prayer and supplication in the Spirit, being watchful to this end with all perseverance and supplication for all the saints" (v. 18).

I believe the most intense battleground in spiritual warfare is the place of prayer, because this is where we do business with God. But prayer is also the most underused weapon in spiritual warfare because it's the hardest thing to do. Most men would rather do anything than pray. Give us a challenge to meet, and we'll meet it. Give us something hard to do, and we'll knock ourselves out trying to accomplish it. But prayer is hard work that requires a different kind of discipline.

The need to pray for our children has never been greater than it is today. Our kids today are facing stuff in elementary and middle school that you and I didn't see in high school. Children need fathers who will engage in "warfare praying" on their behalf.

Ephesians 6:18 is helpful because it tells us to pray for everyone with all kinds of prayers. The best example of praying with all kinds of prayers is the Lord's Prayer that Jesus taught us to pray (Matthew 6:9-13). And since Jesus specifically told us to pray this way, the Lord's Prayer gives us a great outline of the type of prayers we need to be praying for our children.

### Pray for Your Children with Adoration

The Lord's Prayer begins, "Our Father in heaven, hallowed be Your name" (Matthew 6:9). The first kind of prayer you can pray for your kids is a prayer of adoration.

Adoring God and giving Him glory is the place where prayer begins. As a father, then, I pray with adoration and praise to God for the children He has given to Deb and me. The Scripture says, "Children are a heritage from the LORD" (Psalm 127:3), a blessing to a home. When you pray for your children, begin by glorifying God for them, and then pray, "Dear Father, in the name of Jesus Christ I ask You to glorify Yourself through my children and manifest Yourself to the world through our family."

Remember, Dad, that you are the spiritual priest of your family. The primary privilege and responsibility of praying for your children is yours. The patriarch Job is an example of this, as he offered prayers and sacrifices to God on his children's behalf (Job 1:5).

It is also appropriate in adoration to thank the Lord for the people who are having a positive influence on our children, and to praise Him for their growth and spiritual development. Praise God also for the times when He has delivered your children from harm, blessed them, and forgiven them. Spend time giving thanks and hallowing God's name, which means to treat it as holy, as you adore Him for the gift of the children in your home.

*Pray for Your Children with Submission*

Jesus went on to pray in the Lord's Prayer, "Your kingdom come. Your will be done on earth as it is in heaven" (Matthew 6:10). This teaches us to submit our lives to the authority of Jesus Christ and His rule in us.

We must come to the Lord in prayer in a spirit of submission, asking God to rule in the lives of our children. This is where it gets real for us as dads, because so many times we want to shape our kids in our own image. But that's not the goal of parenting. The goal of parenting is to help our children be formed into the image of Christ (Romans 8:29)—first by trusting Him as Savior, then by growing up into the full stature of Christ as mature believers (Ephesians 4:13-16).

The example of Jesus is our example here too. He prayed to His Father in Gethsemane the night before His crucifixion, "Not My will, but Yours, be done" (Luke 22:42). We should be praying the same thing for our children.

I referred above to affirming our children as they pursue God's will. That can be hard for a father who has dreams and plans for his children, particularly his son. But if I truly believe that God knows better than Father what is best for my children, I don't want to be in the position of pushing them in a direction in which God isn't leading them. If you can pray God's will for your children and mean it, regardless of your agenda, you're going to be effective as a praying father.

*Pray for Your Children with Supplication*

"Give us this day our daily bread" is the next part of the Lord's Prayer (Matthew 6:11). This is supplication or petition, asking God for specific needs and requests.

I think all praying dads pray for their children's needs. I also pray for open doors for our children, who are now adults, that God would provide for them along the way. If you have college students, you are probably suffering from "mal-tuition," as we did. But even if your kids are younger, you can begin praying now that God will supply their educational needs.

I also encourage you to pray for your children's future mates. Most fathers with daughters of dating age consider boys to be Neanderthals; one dad said, "I won't mind so much if my daughter brings home a Neanderthal. I just hope he isn't a transitional form!"

Dad, if you want to get real serious in your prayer life real fast, start praying for the young man your daughter will choose someday! Praying with supplication is specific prayer, and I don't know a better topic to be specific about in prayer than life mates for your children.

So many of our prayers are just so general. But when you begin to pray specifically for your family and, in particular, your kids, God begins to move, and you'll see marvelous answers to prayer.

## Pray for Your Children with Confession

We pray with confession when we pray as Jesus taught us, "Forgive us our debts, as we forgive our debtors" (Matthew 6:12).

I can't confess my children's sin, but I can pray that God will lead them to repentance. Our children fail and stumble, as we do, and need God's forgiveness and cleansing. Job prayed on behalf of his children, lest one of them had sinned against God (Job 1:5).

We can also model confession as fathers when we share openly with our children about those times when we have blown it and had to seek God's forgiveness. And sometimes, we need to go to our children and say, "Forgive me, I was wrong." Our children need to know that we live lives of confession and repentance.

## Pray for Your Children with Protection

We've already talked about protecting our children. Jesus prayed, "Do not lead us into temptation, but deliver us from the evil one" (Matthew 6:13a).

The conflict in Iraq is still going on as I write this book. I know many parents of military sons and daughters are praying fervently, and even desperately, for their children's physical protection.

All of us need to pray just as desperately and dependently for our children's spiritual safety, because the "evil one," the devil, is seeking to seduce them and take them for his own. But in prayer we can raise a shield of protection over our children.

### Pray for Your Children with Celebration

The final sentence in the Lord's Prayer is a declaration of God's triumph: "For Yours is the kingdom and the power and the glory forever. Amen" (Matthew 6:13b).

That's something to celebrate! Don't ever forget, we win! Your prayers for your children and your hard work to raise them in the fear and instruction of the Lord are not in vain (read 1 Corinthians 15:58).

I hope your home is a place where God is celebrated. Children often get the idea that prayer is all solemn and serious because they hear adults speak in hushed tones and pronounce words differently, like "Gawwd" instead of "God." But prayer is not a matter of decibels and pronunciation. It is a celebration of our God "who always leads us in triumph in Christ, and through us diffuses the fragrance of His knowledge in every place" (2 Corinthians 2:14).

I believe the members of a home that is bathed in prayer will begin to live in a positive, celebratory spirit. Negative Christianity is a bad advertisement for Jesus Christ, so pray with joy in your heart.

### Pray Constantly for Your Children

Go back to Ephesians 6:18 and notice that we are to pray "always." "Pray without ceasing" (1 Thessalonians 5:17). That doesn't mean that we are on our knees all the time. But it does mean that we have an attitude that is adjusted always to prayer—that we are always just a breath away from prayer. Too many times we pray about something and then quit. But our children are too important for us to quit praying for them.

### Pray Boldly for Your Children

Then we're to pray confidently for our children. Paul said, "Praying always with all prayer . . . in the Spirit" (Ephesians 6:18). There is power when we pray in the Holy Spirit.

If you want to be sure you're praying in the Spirit, pray the Scriptures back to God for your children. He loves to hear His Word! For example, the Bible says, "This is the will of God, your sanctification: that you should abstain from sexual immorality" (1 Thessalonians 4:3).

Turn this clear statement of God's will into a prayer: "Lord, I know it is Your will that my children be sexually pure, and I know You will not lead them into temptation. So I pray with confidence that You will help them avoid temptation and obey You by abstaining from sexual immorality."

### Pray Passionately for Your Children

Finally, we are to pray passionately for our children. Paul said in Ephesians 6:18 that we need to be "watchful" in prayer.

This term refers to a soldier watching at his post. We are to be at our prayer post as though we were in a battle, because we are. We know that Satan is stalking our kids. But we can engage in effective and *victorious* spiritual combat for them through believing prayer, constantly persevering in the name of the Lord Jesus Christ!

# 9

# LIVING A LEGACY FOR YOUR CHILDREN

I REMEMBER WHEN I was playing baseball in high school and college, the track and field team would often be practicing near us. As we stood around waiting our turn to hit during batting practice, I would watch the "thin-clads," as track athletes used to be called because of their lightweight uniforms. I especially liked watching the relay team practice.

It seemed to me that those guys would spend hours and hours just practicing the hand-off, the passing of the baton from one member to the next. There was a reason for that, of course, since the baton hand-off is the most crucial and dangerous moment in a relay race.

You may remember that one of the U.S. women's relay teams messed up the baton hand-off at the 2004 Summer Olympics in Athens, and the team lost the race, even though they were favored to win the gold medal. The absolute shock and agony on those young women's faces said it all in terms of what happens when that hand-off is fumbled.

I don't have to tell you that life is a lot like a relay race, in which you and I are running our "leg" as men, husbands, and fathers who will pass the baton to the next generation. But the wonderful difference between a relay race and life is this: Even though the generation before you may have dropped the baton, you have the opportunity to pass on to your children a godly legacy that will bless them and influence the Kingdom of God for generations to come.

I believe it's time that we begin thinking about this next generation. Many of us "baby boomers" have turned fifty, and some of us are even grandparents. We're hearing a lot about the impact that our generation, the largest in American history, is going to have on things like Social Security when we all hit retirement. One Christian financial expert says we have done the next generation a real disservice because Congress has spent all the money in the Social Security trust fund and there is nothing in the "cookie jar" but a bunch of IOUs.

There isn't much you and I can do about that as individual citizens, but we can make sure that we hand off the baton of faith and commitment to Jesus Christ to our children and grandchildren who are coming right behind us. I want to leave my children a rich spiritual legacy they can draw from and pass on to their children— and I believe you want to do the same.

Psalm 78 describes both our responsibility to leave a legacy of faith and the goal we should be striving for:

> He established a testimony in Jacob, and appointed a law in Israel, which He commanded our fathers, that they should make them known to their children; that the generation to come might know them, the children who would be born, that they may arise and declare them to their children, that they may set their hope in God, and not forget the works of God, but keep His commandments (vv. 5-7).

I like the way the New International Version renders these verses. Here's the heart of it: "He commanded our forefathers to teach their children, so the next generation . . . would put their trust in God and would not forget his deeds but would keep his commands."

If you want to pray a prayer for yourself and your children that will revolutionize your outlook, begin praying Psalm 78 back to the Lord. This is our job description as fathers and grandfathers. We have the awesome privilege and responsibility of teaching the next generation to put their faith and trust in God—to remember the great works of God and obey Him by keeping His commandments.

The question is, how are we going to do this? I believe we do it by *living* a legacy as well as by leaving one. Most people think of a legacy as something we leave behind after we're gone, which often causes us to look backward. But the Bible's emphasis is to look forward and upward, because we have a living faith and we serve a risen, living Savior. If we live the legacy of our faith today, we will be able to pass it on to those who come behind us tomorrow. So how do we live a legacy?

## WE LIVE A LEGACY BY LIVING IN VIEW OF ETERNITY

The Bible calls us to live with the end or goal in mind, which requires that we keep our focus on the race ahead of us. I love the way the writer of Hebrews said it: "Therefore we also [like the heroes of Hebrews 11], since we are surrounded by so great a cloud of witnesses, let us lay aside every weight, and the sin which so easily ensnares us, and let us run with endurance the race that is set before us, looking unto Jesus, the author and finisher of our faith" (Hebrews 12:1-2a).

I appreciate hearing about what God has done in the past, and it's important to know where we came from. And I think it's natural that the older you get, the more you tend to look back. But this is also our time "on the track" to run our portion of the race, and I want to help you make the most of it.

The fact is we have about an eighteen-year window, fewer than two decades, to raise our children and help equip them for the future. And as the father of an empty nest at home, I can tell you that this "window" with children closes so fast you'll get it slammed on your fingers if you're not paying attention! It's just incredible how quickly children grow and go. It is so crucial that we get a handle on the principles and practices of God's Word so we can build a strong spiritual legacy for our families.

## Train Your Children to Love and Serve the Lord

One way to live a legacy for your children is to raise them to honor the Lord and live for something that will far outlive both you and them. The apostle Paul wrote, "And you, fathers, do not provoke your children to wrath, but bring them up in the training and admonition of the Lord" (Ephesians 6:4).

A father who commits himself to teach and train his children in the things of God is looking way down the road, not just to the day when his children will be grown, but to generations yet unborn who will need someone to teach them the truth of Christ.

We've heard it said that God has no grandchildren, only children. The Christian faith is always just one generation from possible extinction—which is both a sobering thought and a tremendous challenge to us to run our part of the race with faithfulness so we can pass the baton of faith to our children.

My friend Steve Farrar has written a book titled *Anchor Man* that speaks to this challenge. He startled me with the thought that one day my children will have grandchildren. But then he took it a step further and said those grandchildren will one day have grandchildren.

Farrar's point is that we should not think of our legacy as simply the seventy or so years we have on earth, or the short time we have while our children are at home. We need to look generations ahead and realize that over the next several hundred years we have an opportunity to change the world through our children and send the message of Christ far into the future.

In fact, we have a special opportunity and challenge today as the fathers who are helping to carry the Christian faith forward into the twenty-first century. Imagine the impact we can have throughout this entire century, if the Lord does not return, if we will rise to the occasion and live a Christ-centered legacy before our families.

## Live with a Passion
## That Your Children Will Catch

No one said it would be easy to be a Christian father and faithful follower of Christ in this generation. One of the challenges of hand-ing off a legacy is that children are not always excited about the same things as their parents. One seminary professor tells his students concerning the teaching of God's Word and the faith of Christ, "If you want other people to bleed, you're going to have to hemorrhage." Someone else said that if you set yourself on fire, some people will at least come to watch you burn.

In other words, if we aren't completely sold out to Jesus Christ and on fire for Him, our children may not catch the real "disease," a passion to live for Christ. I'm told that most fortunes in America are dissipated within one generation of being acquired. What happens is that junior didn't sweat and bleed and watch the pennies to build the business the way dear old Dad did, so spending the fortune is no big deal to him.

There are plenty of challenges and obstacles to overcome in teaching children and instilling in them a commitment to Jesus Christ. But it's exciting to realize that we are not alone in the process. We have the power of the Holy Spirit living within us to give us the ability to live for Christ and to energize our efforts as fathers to pass the faith on to our children.

I never ran a relay race, but I know that one of the worst things a runner can do is to look around or behind him to see where the other runners are. A runner needs to run his own race and keep his eyes focused ahead to the moment when he passes the baton to the next runner.

Paul put it this way in his own life: "One thing I do, forgetting those things which are behind and reaching forward to those things which are ahead, I press toward the goal for the prize of the upward call of God in Christ Jesus" (Philippians 3:13-14). That's living with eternity in view.

Martin Luther, the great Reformer, said, "On my calendar there are only two days, today and that day," the latter referring to the day when Christ would return. Robert Moffatt, one of the great pioneer missionaries, said, "We have all eternity to celebrate our victories, but only one short hour before sunset in which to win them."

That's a great outlook. As believers we are to be looking forward to either the day of Christ's return or the day we go to be with Him. When we make decisions on that basis, every day can become an investment in eternity.

*Get Excited About Heaven and*
*You'll Be More Fruitful on Earth*

Paul is a great example for us. Earlier in his letter to the Philippians, he admitted to being homesick for heaven. He was willing to stay on earth longer because he realized it would mean more fruitful labor. But he really wanted to go to heaven, so he wrote, "I am hard-pressed between the two, having a desire to depart and be with Christ, which is far better" (1:23).

The problem with most of us is that we are willing to go to heaven, but we really want to stay here. We glance at heaven and think about it every so often. But most of our life is focused here and now.

A lot of people are afraid that focusing on heaven and eternity makes us, in these familiar words, "so heavenly minded we're no earthly good."

First of all, I don't think I've ever met anybody who was too heavenly minded. Second, I've met a lot of people who are so earthly minded they're no heavenly good and often wind up being no earthly good, either.

What I'm saying, brother, is that I want you to look far forward into the future and see your children, grandchildren, and great-grandchildren. I want you to ask yourself, "Will the example of faith I am trying to live in my life and pass on to my kids survive into future generations of my family? Am I doing everything today that I can do in order to insure the spiritual future of my family?"

We tend to think there isn't much we can do to influence future generations, but I hope you see that this simply isn't true. If we can lay up treasure in heaven for eternity (Matthew 6:19-21), surely we can live and leave a legacy that will bless our descendants for generations here on earth. Abraham Lincoln once said, "It's not important who our ancestors are, but what our children become."

## Start Living with a Pilgrim Mind-Set

One of my favorite descriptions of a Christian in the New Testament is that of a pilgrim. The writer of Hebrews said that God's heroes "confessed that they were strangers and pilgrims on the earth" (Hebrews 11:13). And Peter wrote to believers as "sojourners and pilgrims" (1 Peter 2:11). We're pilgrims on a journey, because life is not so much a destination as it is a journey. A pilgrim can't afford to keep getting stuck, or getting too comfortable, at various points along the journey or he'll never reach his destination. Life goes on.

Most parents try to teach this principle to their children even concerning the mundane things of life. How many times has an adolescent or a teenager been heartbroken by puppy love, failed to make the team, been embarrassed at school and vowed never to go back, or suffered some other setback that shattered their world? We come alongside at these times and reassure them that this is not the end of the world, and that their lives are not ruined forever. "This too shall pass" is a fact of life.

You may read this and say, "Jack, you're talking about eternity and all that. But I'm just trying to get through next week, much less worrying about my grandchildren's children. I can't handle that kind of responsibility."

Yes, you can, and here's how you do it. Live for Jesus and do the right thing today, and then do the same tomorrow, praying with passion for your family and depending on the power of the Holy Spirit to multiply your investment in the lives of your children. This is the spiritual equivalent of the only proven method for eating an elephant: one bite at a time.

Let me remind you of an encouraging biblical example of a legacy that was lived and passed on with great impact for Christ. The apostle Paul wrote to encourage his son in the faith, Timothy, to be faithful in his ministry at Ephesus despite tough conditions. Paul said he was "filled with joy" (2 Timothy 1:4) when he recalled Timothy's strong spiritual heritage, namely, "the genuine faith that is in you, which dwelt first in your grandmother Lois and your mother Eunice, and I am persuaded is in you also" (v. 5).

Notice the word "genuine" in regard to the faith that had been alive in Timothy's family for three generations. This was authentic faith, without hypocrisy. And the thing I want you to see is that Timothy's mother and grandmother did such a great job that Paul was convinced Timothy's faith was strong enough to keep him going in a challenging ministry.

That's exciting! Wouldn't it be great to have your son or daughter call you one day to say, "Hey, Dad, I just wanted to thank you for the example and heritage you gave me. It's the thing that keeps me going when times are tough."

I can't imagine a better gift for a Christian father to receive—and you can make it happen as you commit yourself to live for Christ every day with your "eyes on the prize"! Don't get so focused on the present that you lose sight of the goal. Transfer your faith to your kids in such a way that they can see your legacy lived out day by day.

## WE LIVE A LEGACY BY LIVING WITHOUT LIMITS

We read earlier in Hebrews 12:1 that we are to "lay aside every weight, and the sin which so easily ensnares us" or slows us down. I like to think of this as a call to live without limits.

The weights here are the encumbrances of life, all the baggage that hangs on us and wears us down. These things may not be sinful, but they are wearisome. And of course, we know how sin can ensnare us and disqualify us from the race or knock us out of the game.

Many athletes wear or carry weights in training and preparation. They used to have ankle weights you could strap on. I'm too far removed from my athlete days to know if those kinds of weights are still used. But the idea is that the weight forces you to work harder and develop muscle so that when you take it off for the big race, you not only feel lighter but are stronger. When it's time for the real competition, a runner strips down to the bare essentials for maximum performance when it matters.

### Lose the Baggage and Run a Strong Race

It's time for us as men, husbands, and fathers who want to make a lasting impact for Christ to strip off the weights and the baggage that drag us down. We need to live without limits, to remove anything and everything in our lives that would keep us from achieving God's best.

We often get sidetracked in this because many of our choices in life are not between good and evil, though we certainly are confronted with those choices, and the options and consequences are pretty clear. But far more often, we must choose between what is good and what is better, or between the better and the best. When I was a young person, adults used to quote this saying: "Good, better, best, never let it rest. Make your good better, and your better best."

Isn't it true that many of the things we chase after so hard turn out to be "trivial pursuits" in light of God's Kingdom? Jesus talked about people who receive the good seed of God's Word, but "the cares of this world, the deceitfulness of riches, and the desires for other things entering in choke the word, and it becomes unfruitful" (Mark 4:19).

Do you ever feel like you're being choked with the cares and the "stuff" of this life? The tyranny of the urgent is always present, and there are plenty of distractions and ultimately trivial pursuits pulling at us. I know you have to earn a living and put food on the table. Someone has to mow the yard and wash the car and paint the house. I'm not saying drop out of the human race, just the rat race. In fact, I'm asking you to crank up the passion and the intensity, and break through the things of earth that so often cause us to live mundane, safe, predictable lives.

## Channel Your Passion into the Things of God

When you think about it, passion is not a problem for most of us. Ted Williams, the late, great Hall-of-Fame ballplayer, said he had one goal in life: "When I walk down the street, I want people to say, 'There goes the greatest hitter who ever lived.'" Williams was so passionate about his hitting that he would go to the bat manufacturing plant to personally oversee the crafting of his bats. He spent countless hours honing his bats and caring for them.

That's passion, but we would have to say in light of eternity that this is an example of a passion for lesser things. You and I have God-given passion and energy that's going to be spent on something, even if it's spent in front of a television set playing "armchair quarterback" for our favorite team.

It really disturbs me to see so many men spending so much passion and energy on things that do not ultimately matter. A large metropolitan area like Dallas offers men many opportunities to invest their passion for life in their careers, homes, or even their cars. The problem is that they not only wind up spending their time in pursuits that are going to perish, but their children pick up on what really matters to them.

I fear a lot of kids today, even in Christian families, are more interested in the Magic Kingdom than they are in the Kingdom of God. There was a famous song in the early 80s called "The Cat's in the Cradle" that hit a lot of fathers right between the eyes. The message of that song was unmistakable: A father who was always too busy to come home and play with his son wakes up one day as a lonely man longing to see his now-grown son, only to find out that his son is too busy for him. I'll tell you, I was a young father then, and that song had a real impact on me.

As I was writing this book, there was a powerful commercial on television that showed a small boy being pushed in a swing and laughing out loud, having the time of his life. You don't really see who is pushing him, but the message that comes on the screen says that the reason they pay extra for overtime is because of all you're missing. The people sponsoring the commercial were making a plea for families to be strong. What a powerful message to dads.

### *Make the Decisions Today*
### *That You'll Be Glad for Tomorrow*

If you're a young father, I believe you really want to be there to push your little boy on the swing at night. I am convinced you want to keep the daily demands and details of life in focus instead of letting them weigh you down and limit your effectiveness for Christ. I believe you want to live to the full for the Lord Jesus Christ without limits, and to teach your children to do the same.

Well, like every other commitment I've addressed in this book, I am equally convinced that this can be done. Now again, if it were easy, everybody would do it. You may have to deny yourself some small pleasures and diversions for the sake of your family. You may even have to make some job and career choices that will allow you more flexibility to pursue what matters most.

I don't know what it would take for you to take off the weights that bog so many guys down and keep them in a rut. But I urge you to do whatever it takes to shed that baggage. You can make a life while you're making a living.

One of the best commitments you can make is simply to lead your family in faithful worship and service in a church where Jesus Christ is exalted and the Bible is believed and taught.

I read a survey not long ago that said when both Dad and Mom take their children to church, 76 percent of those children become active in their faith. When Dad alone takes the children to church, that percentage drops to 55 percent. But when Dad drops out and leaves Mom to take the children to church alone, only 15 percent of those children remain active in their faith. And if neither parent goes to church with the kids, only 9 percent of those kids become active Christians in their church.

Let's focus on that 76 percent. If you heard about an investment that was paying a 76 percent return, you'd be digging in the back of the living room couch for nickels and dimes to scrape together enough money to buy into it. And I'm not talking about anything hard here, just taking your children to church and leading them in worship and service to the Lord. That's a bare minimum of investment in their lives.

But how many fathers can't even disentangle themselves from life or get up enough passion even to take their children to church consistently? Their numbers are legion. Don't let the world limit your focus and your passion to the forty or more hours you put in at the office each week, your favorite hobby, the manicured lawn, or the car in the garage.

Someone has said that we Americans worship our work, work at our play, and play at our worship. What we need is a generation of Christian fathers who will say, starting today, "As for me and my house, we will serve the LORD" (Joshua 24:15).

## We Live a Legacy by Living in the Victory That Is Ours in Christ

I am on a personal campaign to stop whining among believers. "The world's in a mess." "Everything is going to hell. What are we going to do?" "Woe is us. It must be the end times, because many are falling away."

I know that times are tough, and we may indeed be in the end times. But we are children and followers of the King. Our ultimate victory is secure in Jesus Christ. Paul told us to run the Christian race not just so we can stagger across the finish line, but "in such a way that you may obtain [the prize]" (1 Corinthians 9:24; read verses 25-27 to see how to run like a winner).

## Run Your Race Like the Winner You Are in Jesus Christ

I don't know about you, but it sure helps me to run the race knowing that victory is not only possible, but assured! We are not just conquerors, but "more than conquerors through Him who loved us" (Romans 8:37).

Fathers spend a lot of their time cheering for their children in all kinds of events and contests. We yell out encouragement and tell them they can do it and win, even when we know in our hearts that their team is likely going to come out on the short end of the score. How about encouraging your kids in the race of the Christian life, which you can assure them they can win?

Let's pass along to our children not a negative, complaining faith—"Well, you know, kids, this old world is no friend of faith. Jesus was a Man of sorrows, after all. What can you expect?"—but a dynamic, vibrant faith.

You can win as a father, and your children can win too! There was a wonderful human example of this in a story that appeared in *Sports Illustrated* magazine back in 1993.

That year workers were remodeling the Baseball Hall of Fame in Cooperstown, New York. As they moved a cabinet, something fell out that had been hidden behind it. It was a photograph of a middle-aged man in a baseball uniform with the words "Sinclair Oil" on the shirt.

Attached to this photograph was a handwritten note that said, "You were never too tired to play ball. On your days off you helped build the little league field. You always came to watch me play. You were a Hall of Fame dad. I wish I could share this moment with you."

No one had a clue as to who had written this note and placed it and the photo in the Hall of Fame. But *Sports Illustrated* picked up the story and published the photo. A man came forward to say he had written the note about his father. This man, now middle-aged himself, wanted to pay tribute to a dad who had meant so much to him. So he had held a private ceremony in which he inducted his father into the Hall of Fame.

Wow! If that doesn't bring a lump into your throat as a father, you need to check your vital signs. I want to be a Hall of Fame dad, don't you? I want to be in God's Hall of Fame and in my children's Hall of Fame.

I want to close this chapter with a poem titled "The Bridge Builder," by a woman named Will Allen Dromgoole. It's a wonderful call to us as fathers to live and leave a legacy for our children:

An old man, going a lone highway,
Came at the evening, cold and gray,
To a chasm, vast and deep and wide,
Through which was flowing a sullen tide.
The old man crossed in the twilight dim;
The sullen stream had no fears for him;
But he turned, when safe on the other side,
And built a bridge to span the tide.

"Old man," said a fellow pilgrim near,
"You are wasting strength with building here;
Your journey will end with the ending day;
You never again must pass this way;
You have crossed the chasm, deep and wide—
Why build you the bridge at the eventide?"

The builder lifted his old gray head:
"Good friend, in the path I have come," he said,
"There followeth after me today
A youth whose feet must pass this way.
This chasm that has been naught to me
To that fair-haired youth may a pit-fall be,
He, too, must cross in the twilight dim;
Good friend, I am building the bridge for him."

PART FOUR

# A MAN OF GOD
# AND
# HIS MINISTRY

# 10

# THE NEED TO HAVE
# AND TO BE A MENTOR

JOHN WOODEN IS THE LEGENDARY former coach of the UCLA men's basketball team who coached greats like Kareem Abdul-Jabbar and Bill Walton and won ten national college basketball titles.

Wooden was a master teacher who overlooked no detail in helping his players learn the game of basketball and perform at their best. Coach Wooden was said to start each year by showing his players the proper way to lace up their sneakers so their shoes would fit properly during a game.

Like many great coaches, John Wooden also influenced many of his athletes far beyond the athletic arena. The current buzzword that might be used to describe Coach Wooden is "mentor." The term comes from the name of Mentor, a friend of Odysseus in ancient Greece who was charged with the education of Odysseus's son, Telemachus. Thus a mentor is a guide or counselor. One dictionary lists "tutor" and "coach" as synonyms for a mentor.

We could also add words like "husband," "father," "teacher," "supervisor," and several more to this list, describing the roles we are called to fill as men seeking to be men of God. All of us need at least one mentor in our lives, and God in His grace usually gives us several. We also have the opportunity and responsibility to mentor other people God brings into our lives.

As always our textbook for learning what the process of mentoring is all about is God's inerrant Word. The Bible is filled with examples of men who played critical mentoring roles in the lives of others, and it also teaches us what a mentor is and does, and the qualities a mentor needs to be a godly influence.

I have had some important men in my life who invested themselves in me. I think of my grandfather, in whose home we lived when I was a child. My grandfather probably didn't know what the word "mentor" meant, but every evening he would set me on his lap, read the Scripture to me, and talk with me about the things of God or whatever else I wanted to talk about. My grandfather invested his life in me.

My own father was a blue-collar guy who worked many long hours. And yet, when he was off work, my dad gave of himself to me in many life-shaping ways.

I also think of my former pastor, Dr. Fred Swank, in Fort Worth, Texas. Dr. Swank pastored the same church for forty-three years. As a young seminary student he came to a church on the east side of Fort Worth that had a few hundred members and grew it to more than 5,000 members over the years.

One quality I admired so much in Dr. Swank was his faithfulness. His favorite verse was, "Therefore, my beloved brethren, be steadfast, immovable, always abounding in the work of the Lord, knowing that your labor is not in vain in the Lord" (1 Corinthians 15:58).

When I was a teenager, Dr. Swank saw something in me and was willing to give of himself to me. So many of the important decisions I have made in life are a direct result of his influence on my life. Fred Swank was a mentor to me and many other young men whom God called to preach.

It's great to have godly mentors. We benefit immensely from the investment they make in our lives. And when we invest something of ourselves in others, whether it be our own family, friends, or fellow church members, we are depositing something in their lives that will last through the years.

As you grow in your own faith and continue to become a man

of God, I urge you to take someone else with you on your journey of faith. Campus Crusade for Christ used to tell their campus staff members, "Never go anywhere by yourself if you can take a student with you." The idea was to have informal, quality time to build into those students' lives.

That's mentoring. Some churches have formal mentoring programs, but so much of this teaching and coaching takes place in the ordinary routines of life. Of course, if you are a father there is no greater mentoring you could do than to invest your life in your own children.

More people in America are coming to recognize the incredibly damaging effects of fatherless homes. Fatherlessness is the number one predictor of a young man who will be drawn into crime and a host of other problems that are tearing at the fabric of our society. The only way to make a truly lasting difference is to change hearts, and that happens one heart and one life at a time. Dad has the best chance to teach his children the things of God, which is why we need men of God who will seek mentors for themselves and become a mentor to others.

## EVERY MAN NEEDS TO HAVE A MENTOR

My friend John Maxwell writes that we all need different kinds of mentoring along the way. If you have someone you can point to who is fulfilling each of these functions in your life, you are blessed!

### We Need Someone to Encourage Us

Everybody needs an encourager. The best example of an encouraging mentor in Scripture is Barnabas, whose very name meant "Son of Encouragement" (Acts 4:36). Actually, Barnabas was the nickname of this amazing Levite from Cyprus, because his real name was Joses (see v. 36a). He was such a great encourager that it became his identifying trait.

Barnabas was God's cheerleader. When the early church in Jerusalem was in need, Barnabas sold a piece of land and gave the money to the apostles (Acts 4:37) for the saints' needs.

But his greatest work of encouragement was the ministry Barnabas had in the life of Paul. After Paul came to faith in Christ and began to preach the gospel, he had to leave Damascus over the wall in a basket because the Jews were trying to kill him (Acts 9:23-25). Paul came to Jerusalem, but the believers there were afraid to associate with the man who had been Saul, the zealous persecutor of the church (v. 26).

Enter Barnabas. According to Acts 9:27, "Barnabas took [Paul] and brought him to the apostles." Paul gave his testimony, and the church finally believed that he had indeed become a Christian, and they accepted him as a brother.

Then later, when the church at Antioch was experiencing a great outpouring of blessings from God, the Jerusalem church sent Barnabas to Antioch, where he "encouraged them all that with purpose of heart they should continue with the Lord" (Acts 11:23). Barnabas then left Antioch to search for Paul and bring him back (vv. 25-26), and the great apostle became a leading teacher in the church and, soon after that, the church's first and greatest missionary.

I hope you have a Barnabas in your life—someone who believes in you and encourages you to go for God's best and serve Him with gusto. I'm grateful for the people who have been Barnabas-like encouragers to me. We never outgrow our need for encouragement.

## We Need Someone to Confront Us

You and I also need a mentor who will put a finger in our chest when necessary. We need a Nathan, the prophet who confronted David after David committed adultery with Bathsheba, had her husband Uriah killed, and then covered up his sin for months (2 Samuel 11-12).

God sent Nathan to call David to account for his sin, and in so doing Nathan played a critical role in David's life. Nathan's courageous declaration, "You are the man!" (2 Samuel 12:7), set David on the road to repentance and restoration with God. Nathan risked his life to do what he did, for a king in the ancient world held the power of life and death over his subjects. But David came back home spiritually because he had a Nathan to call his hand and not let him drift away from the Lord.

I've got a Nathan in my life, a close friend who isn't afraid to ask me the hard questions and deal with me when I mess up. One of the myths of manhood is the Clint Eastwood type of guy who is tough and rugged and goes his own way, answering to no one. But I pity the man who thinks he is accountable to no one.

### We Need Someone to Teach Us

There's a third kind of mentor every man needs, represented by the apostle Paul and the ministry he had in young Timothy's life. In fact, I believe that in 2 Timothy 2:1-2 we have the ideal description of a mentor: "You therefore, my son, be strong in the grace that is in Christ Jesus. And the things that you have heard from me among many witnesses, commit these to faithful men who will be able to teach others also."

Timothy was Paul's student, his protégé, in the ministry. Paul was the master teacher who imparted solid biblical truth to Timothy, but Paul also imparted his life to Timothy, like a father to his son.

We are going to look more closely at this text and the following verses below, so I'll save most of my comments for that section. But I want you to see how absolutely vital it is that you put yourself under the clear, sound teaching of God's Word.

For many believers, the person who helps to fulfill this role is a pastor or Sunday school teacher. We can also be taught by great Christians of the past by reading and studying their works. Every man needs a Paul, because we should never stop learning and growing, particularly in the things of Christ.

### EVERY MAN NEEDS TO BE A MENTOR

It has been said that every man is a leader and an influencer in some sphere of his life, and I really believe that. Most of us can count at least three areas—family, work, neighborhood—where we interact with and influence others, regardless of whether we carry a formal title of leadership.

If you're reading this book as the sole inhabitant of an island somewhere in the Pacific Ocean, please drop me a note and tell me you're an exception! Otherwise, I think I'm safe in assuming that you have a role to play as a mentor in some person's life. And just as we need an encourager, confronter, and teacher, we also need to fill these roles in the lives of those around us.

## We Need to Encourage Someone

Where did we get the idea that to be an encourager, a person has to have an effervescent, sunny personality and wear a perpetual smile? It's true that these kinds of people are really good at encouragement, and it probably comes more naturally to them than to the rest of us. But that doesn't excuse us from building positive input into other people.

We need to understand the nature of true biblical encouragement. It's not just a slap on the back and a smile that may or may not be real. The ministry Barnabas had to the church at Antioch is a prime example of biblical encouragement. We read it earlier: He "encouraged them all that with purpose of heart they should continue with the Lord" (Acts 11:23).

Real encouragement has content and purpose to it, in other words. This doesn't mean we have to share a Bible verse each time we try to encourage someone, although that would not be a bad idea. But it does mean that we need to know another person well enough, and care enough, to say, "Bob, I know you're struggling with that teenager right now, but hang in there. You're doing the right thing to hold to your standards, and God will bless you for honoring Him."

If you can't think of anyone to encourage, why not start at home? Children need to be raised with two pats—one low enough to correct them when they do wrong, and one high enough to encourage them when they do the right thing. As unbelievable as it seems to most of us, many adults say their fathers never gave them a single word of affirmation or encouragement the entire time they were growing up.

No wonder I see so many lonely Christian men. They have wives and children—they just don't have real friends. Men aren't very good at relationships, which means that many men live in relational solitude. They may work with a lot of people, but they don't have anyone to build them up in their faith. Make it your goal to be a genuine encourager.

## We May Need to Confront Someone

There are also times when we need to be a Nathan to a David who is in trouble and drifting from the faith. So often I see guys disappear from the work of the Lord and the church. And so often, we just let it happen by letting those men go.

I can hear some guy saying, "Are you kidding? There is no *way* I'm going to stick my nose into another guy's business and get it chopped off. Besides, I would have no idea how to do it."

Well, I don't have an easy answer for you, but maybe these thoughts will help. By the way, let me start by relieving you of the notion that confronting people is somehow easy for me because I'm a pastor. Confronting an errant person is one of the hardest things any man has to do, especially if it's another man who needs to be spoken to.

But it has to be done at times, and I believe God will enable us to confront. It's really a matter of caring about others and putting another person's interests and needs ahead of our own (Philippians 2:4).

I like the anti-drug commercials on television that say to young people, "If your friend were in trouble, you'd help him, wouldn't you?" One of them shows a boy on a bike who has fallen in the middle of the road. A big truck is coming around the curve, and the boy is about to be crushed. But his buddy just stands there looking at him, not making any attempt to help. As cruel as that would be, the ad's point is that it's just as cruel to let a friend destroy himself on drugs without trying to help.

Let me say it again. Confronting is caring. And I'm not talking about acting like a Pharisee and going on the hunt for people to rebuke. If someone tells you he has the gift of criticism, proceed immediately to the nearest exit! But if you sense by the Spirit of God that someone you care about is drifting from the Lord or is involved in sin, you owe it to that person to reach out in love and bring him back.

## We Need to Teach Someone

Sometimes I wonder if, when men hear the teaching of the Word in church or some other gathering, they mentally see a disclaimer on the screen like those fine-print disclaimers on a lot of car commercials: "Professional driver on closed course. Do not attempt at home."

I don't know of anything that will put the average guy into a sweat faster than telling him he ought to be teaching others the Word of God. Lots of dads are great teachers if we're talking about showing junior how to swing a bat or change the oil—and there's nothing wrong with that. But the Bible? That's usually another story.

Part of the problem is that many guys have this misconception that because they are not trained theologians, they should leave the teaching to the professionals. Plus, there are a lot of men who have "attempted this at home" in terms of opening the Word with their families and have met with frustration.

But mentoring as a teacher does not necessarily imply a formal time of instruction. You don't have to sit the family down while you expound at length on a text. Just reading the Bible as a family is a great start, and from what I can tell, is more than what many Christian families do on a regular basis.

If you can read, you can teach. You don't have to teach the book of Leviticus. I heard about one poor guy who decided he was going to read the Bible at the dinner table, starting with Genesis. But it wasn't long before he hit one of those Old Testament genealogies. He began stumbling over the names as the kids smirked and Mom tried to look serious while stuffing her napkin in her mouth to keep from laughing.

There's a better way to do it. Pick a verse and discuss it at dinner. Memorize Scripture as a family. That's teaching, Dad, and it ought to start with you. There's something about a father's authority in the home that, when children see Dad is serious about this, they take it more seriously.

I hope you are also part of a men's group that regularly meets for fellowship, accountability, Bible study, and prayer. Small groups give you an opportunity to study the Bible and become more comfortable sharing the Word with others.

## THE QUALITIES A MENTOR NEEDS TO HAVE A GODLY INFLUENCE

I want to come back to 2 Timothy 2 and dig out some of the riches of this text in relation to mentoring. Here Paul borrowed examples from life to teach young Timothy what a mentor is and does. I want to give you some characteristics we need to be developing to be a Barnabas, Nathan, and Paul to others.

Let's remember that the ultimate bottom line of our mentoring is not just to teach our children life lessons they need, or to help a friend. We're talking about passing along faith in Jesus Christ. Paul told Timothy, "That good thing which was committed to you, keep [or guard] by the Holy Spirit who dwells in us" (2 Timothy 1:14).

This "good thing" is the same as "the things" (2 Timothy 2:2) Paul had taught Timothy—the truths of God's Word. As I said earlier, our mentoring must be built around real content, the Word of God and the testimony of faith in Jesus Christ. The payoff comes when we commit the truth to "faithful men," who then go out and pass the faith along. This is how the church of Jesus Christ has grown through the generations and the centuries.

Our tendency seems to be that each succeeding generation wants to "dumb down" in terms of our commitment to Scripture. Today many churches are trying to accommodate the culture by weakening the message of Christ. But the Word of God doesn't change or go out of style. The apostle Jude told us, "Contend earnestly for the faith which was *once for all* delivered to the saints" (Jude 3, emphasis added).

That's why Paul said to commit these things to "faithful men," as opposed to unfaithful men who doubt or even deny the accuracy and sufficiency of Scripture. It's vital that we commit ourselves as men and mentors to God's Word—not only to hear it, but to heed it.

### A Mentor Must Be Strong in the Faith

In verses 1 and 3-6 of 2 Timothy 2, Paul mentioned several traits that help us see what makes a good mentor. The first of these is in verse 1, where he told Timothy, "My son, be strong."

Weak churches and weak families are a result of weak leaders. We have popular churches today, but very few powerful churches. We have popular preachers today, but not very many powerful ones. It's up to us to be strong in the faith.

"My son, be strong" was written as a command. Apparently one of Timothy's problems was a natural timidity. Earlier Paul had written, "God has not given us a spirit of fear, but of power and of love and of a sound mind" (2 Timothy 1:7). Paul was constantly building Timothy up and strengthening him. He wanted Timothy to grow strong spiritually.

Being an effective mentor requires that the grace of God be continually at work in us. There are times when I am weak, but the grace that is working in me enables me to do what I could not do in my own strength. There is no reason for any child of God to feel inadequate. Peter said that God has given us "all things that pertain to life and godliness" (2 Peter 1:3).

Sometimes you hear guys say, "Well, I just sort of serve the Lord in my own weak little way."

Well, stop it! Stop serving God in your weak way and start serving Him in His mighty, powerful way through the Holy Spirit who lives in you. Paul had, no doubt, shared with Timothy the truth of

Philippians 4:13: "I can do all things through Christ who strengthens me." So be strong as God's son. Let's grow up and be mature as men and mentors.

## A Mentor Must Be Disciplined in Lifestyle

Paul continued in his instructions to Timothy: "You therefore must endure hardship as a good soldier of Jesus Christ. No one engaged in warfare entangles himself with the affairs of this life, that he may please him who enlisted him as a soldier" (2 Timothy 2:3-4).

Even when a soldier is on leave, he's still a soldier. If you were in Israel today, you might see a young man in civilian clothes walking along a highway with a rifle slung over his shoulder. He would probably be an Israeli soldier going back to base after being home on leave. You can also see soldiers at bus stops and around town in Jerusalem, always carrying their weapons even if they're not in uniform. Israel is on round-the-clock alert for attack, so soldiers there must always be ready to defend themselves. And one look at an Israeli army training base in the desert will tell you this is no summer camp. Those soldiers endure hardship, and they're as tough as nails.

Israel's military conditions are a great illustration of what Paul was talking about. Sometimes I wonder what is going to happen to our generation of weak-kneed, candy-legged Christian "soldiers" when the heat gets turned up. And I'm not just pointing a finger at others. I dare say none of us has suffered all that much for being a Christian. I've been blessed beyond measure.

But the fact remains that we are called to endure hardship for Christ. Most guys I know don't want to follow a mentor who has to say, "Now, I've never really been through this, but I want to tell you how to get through it."

A friend who was drafted into the army during the Vietnam conflict said he and his company were sitting in a class one day while the nastiest drill sergeant in the outfit showed them how to disassemble, clean, and reassemble an M-16 rifle. My friend said they had been in basic training for only a week or so and were still in shock. The room was stuffy, it was the middle of the afternoon, and the last thing these young men wanted to know that day was how to clean a rifle. No one was paying attention, and some were drifting off into dreamland.

But all of a sudden the drill sergeant stopped, slammed his big fist on the table, and shouted angrily at the troops to wake up. Among other things that can't be repeated, he told those new soldiers, "Listen up, you knuckleheads! Knowing how to handle this weapon may just save your life someday in Vietnam. I've done my time over there, and now it's your turn, so listen up!"

My friend said hearing the words "Vietnam" and "save your life" in the same breath snapped him back to reality. He and his buddies sat up and hung on every word the sergeant said. Now he had information they desperately wanted because he had been there and knew what he was talking about, and they might have to face the same thing. He ceased being just a drill sergeant at that point and became a very effective mentor!

A soldier has to endure not only hardship, but separation. Soldiers can't afford to get entangled in civilian affairs. It makes them, to use the apostle James's famous words, "double-minded" and "unstable in all [their] ways" (James 1:8).

Brother, we need to remind ourselves that we are not of this world. We are twice-born men in a once-born world! The order from our Commander in Chief is, "Come out from among them and be separate" (2 Corinthians 6:17). A soldier leaves regular society behind because he is a man who hears a different drummer.

## A Mentor Must Be Rigorous in Training

To be good mentors, we must also train like athletes going for the gold. In Paul's next illustration, he wrote, "And also if anyone competes in athletics, he is not crowned unless he competes according to the rules" (2 Timothy 2:5).

The word *compete* means to "wrestle" or "struggle." It's the picture of a determination to win! Paul said elsewhere, "Run in such a way that you may [win]" (1 Corinthians 9:24). Just as an athlete strives for the prize, if we're going to be mentors who can teach others and pass the faith along, we need to be in training and stay in top form.

If the late football coach Vince Lombardi could say, "Winning isn't everything, it's the only thing," then I think we as followers of Jesus Christ should have the same passion to win for Him. Later in 2 Timothy, Paul declared, "I have fought the good fight, I have finished the race, I have kept the faith" (4:7). The reason more people don't win in the Christian life is that they are not willing to pay the price of victory.

Notice also that we must compete according to the rules. The steroid controversy in major league baseball was just unfolding as this book was being written. Some big-time stars have had a lot of the luster scratched off their shine. Any boy in a ballgame can tell you it doesn't really count if you cheat.

Paul was afraid of being disqualified for breaking the rules. "I discipline my body and bring it into subjection, lest, when I have preached to others, I myself should become disqualified" (1 Corinthians 9:27). Paul lived with the dread that somehow he would disqualify himself from the race and be benched because Jesus Christ could no longer use him.

I know men who formerly were faithful to the Lord, but they ran out of bounds, so to speak. They broke the rules, and God is not using them today. I challenge you to maintain your moral and spiritual purity as you strive for the prize. A mentor must be Exhibit A of the principles he wants to instill in others.

## A Mentor Must Be Hardworking in Dedication

The last metaphor Paul used is a farmer: "The hardworking farmer should be the first to receive a share of the crops" (2 Timothy 2:6, NIV).

I think "hardworking farmer" is a needless redundancy. The only farmers who don't work hard are ex-farmers. I grew up in town and have never lived on a farm. But I saw how hard farmers work and sweat when I went to a little town called Hobart in southwestern Oklahoma to be a pastor.

The community was made up of Dutch-German wheat farmers, and I learned to live and die with the wheat harvest each year. I watched those farmers get up early and stay up late year-round. Farming is not something they did part-time. It takes hard work to be a farmer, and they are often unheralded. Soldiers get medals and athletes get trophies. Farmers get calluses.

Paul said to Timothy, "Be willing to work hard like a farmer." Not everyone can stand in the spotlight with a trophy in his hand. But like a hardworking farmer, all of us can find a job to do in God's harvest fields and do it. We must be willing to spend and be spent for Christ.

God's Word to us as mentors is, "Pass the faith along to faithful men who will be mature, strong sons, soldiers ready for spiritual warfare, athletes striving for the prize, and hardworking farmers for the cause of Christ."

## IT'S AMAZING WHAT A FAITHFUL MENTOR CAN ACCOMPLISH

One of my favorite mentoring stories begins with a man named Edward Kimball, who lived in Boston in the mid-1850s. Kimball was a dedicated Sunday school teacher who loved the Lord.

One day Kimball felt the Lord prompting him to visit one of his students, a young salesman in a local shoe store. Kimball obeyed that leading, even though he was nervous as he shared the gospel with young Dwight Moody. Moody accepted Christ that day in the back of the shoe store.

Not long after that, Dwight Moody moved on to Chicago where he established a great work for the Lord. And in 1872, Moody and his musician partner, Ira Sankey, sailed to Great Britain where Moody turned the British Isles upside down and became the greatest evangelist of the nineteenth century.

On one occasion, Moody preached in a cold, dead, dried-up church whose pastor, Frederick Meyer, was about to quit. But when this pastor heard Moody preach and saw the power and conviction in his life, God did a fresh work in this young pastor's heart that changed the course of his ministry. He became a powerful preacher of the gospel and wrote many books that have influenced generations of believers. He is better known as F. B. Meyer, and I would say, even today, if you find a book by him, get it and read it.

After his contact with Moody changed his ministry, Meyer came to America and preached in a seminary in Pennsylvania. It was a rather liberal school, and there was a young student there who was about to bail out on preparing for the ministry. He had concluded that if what he was seeing and experiencing was Christianity, he didn't want to give his life to it.

But when this seminary student heard the great F. B. Meyer preach the Word with authority in the power of the Holy Spirit, he recommitted his life to the ministry. His name was Wilbur Chapman, and he too became a mighty preacher of the gospel and an evangelist who traveled all across this country.

Soon a professional baseball player who had been powerfully converted to Christ and felt a call to ministry started following Chapman around. This young man, an outfielder for the Chicago White Sox, gave up his baseball career to travel with Wilbur Chapman and help the great evangelist in any way he could.

One day Wilbur Chapman told his young assistant, "I'm going to be a pastor. Son, I want you to take over this ministry and be an evangelist." And that's exactly what Billy Sunday did, becoming the most powerful evangelist in America in the early decades of the twentieth century. Sunday led countless people to Christ, preaching with power and great impact as he used his athletic ability and even some theatrics to dramatically illustrate his messages.

As Billy Sunday's ministry drew to a close, a lesser-known man named Mordecai Ham took up his mantle and became an evangelist. A group of farmers in Charlotte, North Carolina, who had been praying for revival in their community, wanted to hold a crusade and invited Billy Sunday to come. But Sunday couldn't come, so these farmers decided to invite Mordecai Ham instead. As they prepared for the crusade, they prayed, "Lord, send us a revival that will change the world."

One night a tall, lanky seventeen-year-old North Carolina boy came to hear Mordecai Ham. He had to sit in the choir loft because there wasn't any room for him on the floor of the tabernacle. So a teenaged Billy Graham listened to Ham, then came back the next night and gave his life to Christ. And indeed, the revival those North Carolina farmers prayed for has changed the world through Dr. Graham.

Brother, that's how mentoring works! Not many people know the name of Edward Kimball, but when all these servants of Christ I named are rewarded for their accomplishments for Christ, Edward Kimball is going to be at the head of the line—a faithful Sunday school teacher who obeyed the Spirit of God and passed his faith on to a young Dwight L. Moody. God help us to do that today!

# 11

# SHARING OUR LORD, OUR LIGHT, AND OUR LABOR

A POLICE DETECTIVE MADE an unusual discovery several years ago in Plano, Texas, the city in which our church is located.

As far as anyone knew, the Plano police department had never lost an officer in the line of duty. But this detective discovered some old records that piqued his interest in the story of G. W. Rye, who was shot to death during a bank robbery in Plano in 1920 at the age of 52, leaving a wife and children behind.

The original report of the robbery called Mr. Rye a "night watchman," which made him appear to be a private security guard. But another old clipping referred to him as a sworn peace officer, with a badge and weapon and arrest authority. So the detective began a painstaking investigation on his own that convinced him Mr. Rye was indeed a Plano police officer.

The detective eventually located surviving members of the slain officer's family and was excited to learn they still had his badge. When the detective asked them what was inscribed on the badge, the answer came back: "Police, Plano, Texas."

With the late officer's true status verified, G. W. Rye was duly honored in our city and inducted into the Texas Peace Officers

Memorial in May 2003, an honor he and his family richly deserve. It didn't matter to this detective that Officer Rye's death occurred many years ago. He said it was "a big deal" to find out that Mr. Rye was a police officer, and he said the story is an important part of Plano's history.

Police officers are a very close-knit brotherhood, and every member suffers when one member falls in the line of duty. They will even go out of their way and spend their own time to see that a fallen brother officer receives the honor he is due.

My hope and prayer is that the people of God, the church of Jesus Christ, and particularly men who are followers of Jesus Christ, will be that committed to one another and to the great cause for which we are giving our lives—spreading the gospel of Jesus Christ and building His Kingdom.

We certainly have much to knit us together. We learned earlier that the great New Testament word for this shared life is *koinonia*, which comes from a word meaning "common" or "shared." We may have different backgrounds, but we are one body in Christ. As my friend Dr. Tony Evans says, "We may have come over here on different ships, but we're in the same boat now."

Jesus is the One who binds us together. We are one in the bond of His life and in the beauty of His love. The apostle John said he was writing down what he had seen and heard about Jesus, "that you also may have fellowship [*koinonia*] with us; and truly our fellowship is with the Father and with His Son Jesus Christ. And these things we write to you that your joy may be full" (1 John 1:3-4). We share a common Lord, a common light, and a common labor as brothers in Christ.

## WE SHARE A COMMON LORD

What makes the church different from any organization on earth is the Lord Jesus Himself. What makes us different from a club or a lodge is what we believe about Him. We can have fellowship, or true sharing, with God the Father and with Jesus because Jesus is the Lord of all and the Lord of us all.

## *Jesus Christ Is the Preeminent Lord*

Of course, when we say Jesus is our "common" Lord, we are not using that word in its everyday meaning. There is nothing ordinary about Jesus. He is the preeminent Lord of heaven and earth!

John began his first epistle with these words: "That which was from the beginning, which we have heard, which we have seen with our eyes, which we have looked upon, and our hands have handled, concerning the Word of life." That's Jesus. He is the Giver and Sustainer of life as well as our Savior and sovereign Lord. Jesus is eternal Lord and eternal God.

## *Jesus Christ Is a Physical Lord*

The fact that Jesus left the glory and dignity of heaven to take on the indignity of human flesh is at the heart of our faith. John said in the verse above that his eyes saw Jesus, and his hands touched Him. Jesus was not an angel or a spirit who only appeared to take on human flesh, as some have taught throughout church history.

The Gnostics, whose name is taken from the Greek word for knowledge, were the heretics of John's day. They taught that physical matter was evil and spirit was good, which made it impossible that God could become a material being and take on human flesh.

In battling these heretics, John declared, "No, it's true. Jesus had a real body. We saw Him with our own eyes, we heard Him, we touched Him. He was not a phantom."

The word translated "seen" in 1 John 1:1 comes from the Greek word for "theater." Jesus appeared on the stage of history in the drama of redemption, and the apostles and many others were the audience who saw Him.

The irreducible core of the Christian faith is this: Jesus became one of us so that we might be one with Him. He was born of a virgin and lived a sinless life. Then He died on the cross, the Just One for the unjust ones, to redeem us.

Jesus is the God-Man, and He always will be. Even now in heaven, Jesus bears in His glorified body the scars of the flesh. His scars are the only manmade thing in heaven. We will see those scars to remind us forever of what Christ did for us.

### Jesus Christ Is a Personal Lord

This is another central truth of the Christian faith. We can know Christ in a personal relationship that can be closer than any human, earthly relationship.

In Revelation 3:20, Jesus described Himself as standing outside the door of His church, seeking to gain entrance so He can have fellowship with His people. Jesus seeks intimacy of communion and fellowship with each member of the church, which is His very body. Hebrews 2:11 says Jesus is not ashamed to call us His "brethren," or brothers, a term of deep fellowship and affection. This is why I can say that Jesus is not only the Savior of the church, but He is *my* Savior.

This is why the church is all about Jesus. My brother, if you are not in a church that is all about Jesus, you need to get into one where He is exalted above all. You need to involve yourself in a church where Christ is worshiped as the preeminent, physical, and personal Lord who wants to share His life with His people. We share a common Lord.

## WE SHARE A COMMON LIGHT

Another commonality of our faith is that we share a common light. John continued in 1 John 1: "This is the message which we have heard from Him and declare to you, that God is light and in Him is no darkness at all. If we say that we have fellowship with Him, and walk in darkness, we lie and do not practice the truth. But if we walk in the light as He is in the light, we have fellowship [*koinonia*] with one another, and the blood of Jesus Christ His Son cleanses us from all sin" (vv. 5-7).

I don't even have to ask you if you have ever tried to walk in the darkness. Every man has at one time or another. It must be part of our hunter instinct—or maybe we're just too lazy to go over and turn on the light. But any man worth his salt as a father or husband has scars from encountering coffee tables or stepping bare-footed on roller skates or miniature metal cars while trying to walk through the house in the dark. We need to turn on the light to keep from stumbling around and falling.

It's foolish and painful to walk around in darkness when you don't have to, and spiritually it can be fatal. Praise God that Jesus has brought us out of the darkness and into His marvelous light!

One way you know you are saved is that you have moved from darkness into the light. Things that didn't matter at all suddenly become very important because you see them in their true light for the first time. The darkness that engulfed your mind and heart are lifted, and you can walk without stumbling. Jesus declared, "I am the light of the world. He who follows Me shall not walk in darkness, but have the light of life" (John 8:12). It's wonderful to step out of the darkness into the light—and even more wonderful to discover many brothers and sisters who have also come to the light of Jesus Christ. We share the close connection of being followers of the same light.

## WE SHARE A COMMON LABOR

I want to spend some extra time in this third section of the chapter because we are talking about a man of God and his ministry. The church is not only a place to believe and a place to belong, but it is a place to become what God has called us to be, which is ministers, heralds, and servants of the gospel. Therefore, we share a common labor.

Please don't miss this. God has connected us in Christ in order that we might share Him and serve Him. The primary vehicle and voice for doing that is through His body on earth, which is His church.

If you were to ask most people how many ministers they have at their church, they would tell you how many people are on the paid ministerial staff. But that's a trick question, because every member of the church is called to be a minister of Christ. That word means "servant," not paid professional. And all of us are going to stand before Christ one day and give an account of our ministry for Him.

Alan Redpath is a well-known British devotional writer and pastor who said that his conscience was stabbed awake one day when he heard a preacher make this statement: "You can have a saved soul, but a lost life."

Redpath said, "When I heard that, I realized that while I was on my way to heaven, I wasn't taking people to heaven with me. While I realized that I was saved, my life was not influencing others for Christ. I wasn't serving God." He determined in his heart and mind not to waste his life, but to serve God with his body, mind, soul, and strength.

There is a level of fellowship with Christ and with each other that we can enjoy only when we are serving Him in partnership with other members of His body. True fellowship is not doughnuts and coffee, although having those is fine. True fellowship is our commonality in Christ, our commitment to Him and to one another to serve Him together.

## God Has Given Us Tools to Serve Him

Perhaps it has been a while since you took stock of your life and realized the various ways in which God has fashioned and equipped you for service. Some people have gifts that are unique to them, but everybody has the ability to serve God in some fashion.

This reminds me of a hilarious story told by Tommy Lasorda, the former manager of the Los Angeles Dodgers. Lasorda once had a second baseman named Steve Sax, a pretty good ballplayer who could not seem to throw the ball from second to first base with any consistent accuracy.

Sax's erratic throwing was driving Lasorda crazy, so the manager put his arm around Sax one day and walked him out to second base for a fatherly chat.

"Son," Lasorda began in an exasperated voice, "you're hitting about .290. Do you know how many people can hit .290 in the big leagues? Not many. And you've stolen about thirty bases.

Do you know how many people can steal thirty bases? Not many. But you can't throw the ball from second to first. Do you know how many people can throw the ball from second to first? Thousands! My *mother* could throw the ball from second to first! So get with it."

Putting this in spiritual terms, not all of us can sing or write or lead, but all of us can throw the ball from second to first base and play our part in the work of the church.

The apostle Paul reminded us that though there are "diversities of gifts" among the members of Christ's body (1 Corinthians 12:4), "one and the same Spirit works all these things [the gifts], distributing to *each one* individually as He wills" (v. 11, emphasis added).

I'm sure you have heard it said that every true believer in Christ has at least one spiritual gift. No one is left out. People may make jokes about having been behind the door when the good looks or singing ability or some other trait was given out, but no Christian can say he or she was overlooked in the distribution of spiritual gifts. When the Holy Spirit took up residence in your life, the moment you trusted Christ, He did not come empty-handed. He came bearing gifts.

Spiritual gifts, called *charismata* in the Greek language, are ministry gifts, designed not primarily for our enjoyment but for our employment! These are supernatural gifts given sovereignly by God, and each one is different. If you have not already done so, I urge you to discover, develop, and deploy your spiritual gift(s) for the church and the cause of Christ.

And by the way, the nature of spiritual gifts reveals our connectedness. None of these gifts has been designed by God to be exercised in splendid isolation. A lot of men love to think of themselves as rugged individualists, but even the Lone Ranger had Tonto. Roy Rogers had Dale Evans and Pat Brady, Red Ryder had Little Beaver, and Wild Bill Hickok had Jingles P. Jones. There is no solo performer in the body of Christ.

You may have the gift of teaching, but if there aren't some other believers in your church with the gift of service, you may find the door to your Sunday school room locked on Sunday morning, or find the room empty of chairs and tables!

God has also given us a passion for ministry. This is what revs us up and makes us jump out of bed in the morning. I would encourage you to ask yourself, "What is my passion? What do I enjoy doing?" The answer to those questions can help you discover and develop your spiritual gifts.

Let me dispel a common misconception here. Many Christians have the idea that if they enjoy doing something and are good at it, it can't be the will of God for them, because God's will has to be something hard that they don't really want to do.

Where did we ever get that idea? If God gives you a passion for some portion of His service, that's probably a clue that He wants you to serve there! If He has given you a dream to accomplish something for His glory, get with it! Those God-given dreams are what ignite us for spiritual ministry.

Another aspect of God's equipping of us for service is our natural human abilities. There is no spiritual gift of singing or coaching, for example, but these and other abilities can be used to advance the cause of Christ. All of us bring abilities to the table.

I love the way one older gentleman with a kind heart and a warm spirit describes his ministry as a greeter at his church: "I just smile them in and smile them out."

God bless him!

We also get clues and direction for our ministry by the personality and temperament God has given us. If you're not an extrovert, you may be uncomfortable in a ministry that puts you in front of people all the time.

Our ministry is also forged by the things that have happened to us. My father was murdered when I was just nineteen years of age. I was a young preacher preparing for the ministry, and my father's death dramatically affected the formation of my life in ministry. I believe it made me a better comforter of people.

Deb's father also passed away during that same period of time.

We had been married less than two years, and we were both without our fathers whom we loved and needed. My mother passed away five years after my dad. I believe she died of a broken heart. Both of my parents were in their fifties when they were taken from us suddenly. Deb and I grew up in a hurry in terms of experiencing sorrow. And yet, I believe God used those things to help us serve others.

You may come from a broken home. That experience can prepare you for a ministry to others. You may have dealt with divorce or lost your job. I don't know what you've gone through, but whether it is good or bad, all of it can be used to prepare you to reach out to others whose pain you can understand. Bring your wounds to Jesus, and use your scars and tears as a testimony to His grace.

The Bible makes a great statement about Mary of Bethany, Jesus' beloved friend who sat at His feet to hear His words (Luke 10:38-42). Jesus came to the house of Mary, Martha, and Lazarus in Bethany on His way to Jerusalem and the cross, and Mary anointed Jesus with her alabaster box of perfume.

I'm sure Mary and her siblings would have done anything they could for Jesus. You'll remember that some who saw this act of devotion criticized Mary for what they saw as a waste of good perfume. But Jesus rebuked them: "Let her alone. . . . She has done what she could" (Mark 14:6, 8).

Can you do what you can do? You say, "Of course I can do what I can do. What kind of a question is that?" You're right. It seems like a weird question. My real question is, are you *doing* for Jesus what you can do for Him? Mary did what she could. Jesus doesn't ask us to do more than we are able to do.

### God Has Told Us How to Serve Him

It's great to have gifts and abilities and life experiences with which to serve God. But all these things are rendered useless if we try to serve Him with an attitude of arrogance or indifference, selfishly seeking our best instead of the good of others, or treating our ministry for Christ as something to be approached casually or haphazardly.

God's Word tells us how to serve Him. One example is in

Romans 12:1. I call this God's prayer for us—if we can speak of God praying—delivered through Paul. You may have memorized this verse: "I beseech you therefore, brethren, by the mercies of God, that you present your bodies a living sacrifice, holy, acceptable to God, which is your reasonable service."

How are we to serve God? First of all, we serve Him *gratefully* because of all that He has done for us. The word "by" in Romans 12:1 can be translated "because of" God's mercies to us.

Think about what Jesus has done for you. Romans 12 follows on the heels of Paul's great doctrinal treatment of the truth that in Christ, God has brought us from sinful depravity and judgment to the love and grace of God. That's why chapter 12 begins with a "therefore." In light of God's mercy to us in Christ, can we do less than offer Him our lives in full consecration? Of course not. In fact, anything less is downright ingratitude. It's not even reasonable.

Think about this. Giving our lives to Christ is not really giving Him something He doesn't have. We already belong to Him because He has bought us at the price of His blood.

If you looked out your window one day and saw your neighbor trying to get into your car, you would run out and find out what was going on. Suppose he said, "Well, I just decided I like this car, and we want to take it on our vacation."

Even though you are a man of God, you would probably say, "Sorry. I don't know where you got that idea, but I own this car. I paid for it, and I have the papers to prove it. You have no right to pretend this car belongs to you."

I wonder if when we get to heaven, Jesus is going to say to some of us, "Where did you get the idea that your life was yours to do whatever you wanted with? I bought you, and I have the scars to prove it."

Years ago I wrote these words in my Bible. It's simply titled, "The Man God Uses":

He has but one great purpose in his life. He has by God's grace removed every hindrance from his life. He has placed himself absolutely at God's disposal. He has learned how to prevail in prayer. He is a student of the Word. He has a vital, living message for the lost world. He is a man of faith who expects results, and he works in the anointing of the Holy Spirit.

When I was a young pastor, I began praying that God would use me, and I'm grateful for any way He has answered that prayer. We are to serve God gratefully.

We are also to serve God *confidently*, in His power. "I can do all things through Christ who strengthens me" (Philippians 4:13). "Those who wait on the LORD shall renew their strength; they shall mount up with wings like eagles, they shall run and not be weary, they shall walk and not faint" (Isaiah 40:31).

Sometimes we get exhausted, but in Christ we are renewed every day. We may be tired *in* the work of Christ, but we don't get tired *of* the work when we are called of God, because even in our weakness we are made strong. In fact, that's when we're the strongest, as Paul said in 2 Corinthians 12:9-10.

We think, "God will use me when I'm really strong." Well, God uses us most effectively when we present our gifts, abilities, and all we are to Him in dependence and, yes, even in weakness. God can take even our weaknesses, failures, and defeats to accomplish something good for His glory.

The patriarch Jacob had a strength: his ability to deceive people. He was a conniver and was on the run, trying to escape the trouble he had caused. But finally he came to Peniel in total exhaustion, out of tricks and out of options. The Bible says in Genesis 32:24-32 that Jacob wrestled with the angel of the Lord, who had to cripple Jacob to get him to let go!

From that day forward, Jacob limped as a reminder of that encounter. But he received God's blessing, and his life was never the same. And when Jacob appears in God's Hall of Fame in Hebrews 11, what do we read about this great man of faith? He "lean[ed] on the top of his staff" (v. 21) because he had been broken, and yet blessed, at Peniel.

There are no people who are too small for God to use, but there are some people who think they're too big for God to use. Let God use you even in your weakness.

We also need to serve God *sacrificially*. We read it in Romans 12:1. We are to offer ourselves to God as a "living sacrifice." Someone said the problem with a living sacrifice is that it keeps crawling off the altar. Yet we are to put ourselves on the altar of sacrifice and surrender every day.

Service that doesn't cost you anything isn't worth much. Paul described himself as a "servant," literally a "slave" of Jesus Christ (Romans 1:1). The late Dr. Bill Bright, who founded Campus Crusade for Christ, influenced perhaps more people on earth than any one individual in this generation. He did it by reproducing himself in others and raising up an army of witnesses. I'm on a global pastors network with Campus Crusade for Christ, and whenever we would talk with Dr. Bright, someone would inevitably begin complimenting him for this or that achievement. But Dr. Bright would always stop the speaker and say, "Remember this, I'm just a slave of Jesus Christ."

That's the secret of greatness, that we kneel in order to rise. When you're a slave, no task is too small or beneath your dignity. Jesus Himself said, "Even the Son of Man did not come to be served, but to serve" (Mark 10:45).

Are you serving Christ sacrificially? Are you willing to pay the price to serve? Everybody wants to be a leader, but not very many want to be a servant.

And finally, we are to serve Christ *faithfully*. Let's finish what we start, keep our promises, and fulfill our ministries.

Many churches pay a heavy price because their volunteers, their servants, are not faithful. They either don't prepare, or just don't show up. I'm afraid many Christians treat God's work in a way they wouldn't think of treating their job. Try not showing up at work all week without calling in to tell someone where you are or why you're not there, and see what happens.

A man of God is also a man of honor in terms of honoring his commitments. The real heroes in God's Kingdom are the faithful servants who may not be seen and may not receive the applause, but who are there because they are doing their ministry for an audience of One.

Let me remind you of God's requirements for His stewards: "It is required in stewards that one be found faithful" (1 Corinthians 4:2). Jesus' commendation to the servant who pleases Him is, "Well done, good and *faithful* servant" (Matthew 25:21, emphasis added).

We don't read anything in this passage about great talents or gifts, only great faithfulness. That should be encouraging to all of us, for while there will always be someone around who is more gifted or talented than we are, we can be the best at being faithful.

It's a lifetime assignment for us to serve God gratefully, confidently, sacrificially, and faithfully—but we can do it in the power of the Holy Spirit. And we can encourage each other along the way, because we are not in competition for some prize that only one person can win. We share a great Lord, a great light, and a great labor, and someday we will all share in the reward of serving Him.

# 12

# A COMMISSION TO MARKETPLACE EVANGELISM

A FEW YEARS AGO, a powerful series of tornadoes struck Oklahoma City and several surrounding communities. In the town of Moore, people emerged from the storms to find their houses in rubble and everything dark. People were wandering around in the darkness looking for family members and friends.

Rescue and first aid personnel needed a base of operations, so they took huge spotlights and shone them on the cross atop the steeple of the First Baptist Church of Moore. Then they took megaphones and went up and down the streets, shouting, "Follow the light to the cross and you'll find help there!"

That is one of the finest illustrations of evangelism I have found in a long time. We cannot keep people from being lost and from dying, but we can shine our light on the cross of Jesus Christ and urge the lost to run to Him. A commitment to evangelism is part of what it means to be a man of God, and the best place for us to carry out evangelism is in our marketplace.

I'm using that term the way the ancient Greeks used it. Their lives revolved around the *agora*, or "marketplace," which was not only the center of commerce and business but also the place of trade and shopping and the focus of everyday life where people from all walks of life gathered. Marketplace is a great shorthand term for the spheres of life in which you spend most of your time, including your place of work.

We need a commitment to evangelism, but I titled this chapter "A *Commission* to Marketplace Evangelism" because there is more involved here than just our will. We are men under orders, men on a mission for Christ because He has given us our "marching orders." Jesus commanded us, "Go therefore and make disciples of all the nations, baptizing them in the name of the Father and of the Son and of the Holy Spirit, teaching them to observe all things that I have commanded you; and lo, I am with you always, even to the end of the age" (Matthew 28:19-20).

Notice the progression here. We are to *make* disciples, then we are to *mark* them as disciples through believer's baptism, and finally we are to *mature* those disciples by teaching them the things of Christ.

This is called the Great Commission, and it is the whole job of the whole church. Not all of us are in a position where we can baptize people, and not all of us can be teachers. But we can all be evangelists—and in fact, that is part of our calling as believers. "Do the work of an evangelist," the apostle Paul told Timothy, his son in the faith (2 Timothy 4:5). Sharing Christ with others is His clear command and commission for us. We are commissioned to share the faith we hold in Jesus Christ.

Some guys object by saying, "Wait a minute. I can't do that. I'm not a professional. I don't do well in public speaking."

You don't have to be a polished speaker or a theologian to share your faith. All you have to do is tell someone else what Jesus did for you and how they can know Him too. Someone said evangelism is just one beggar telling another beggar where to find bread.

I like to think of evangelism as a person who has been cured of a terminal disease being so excited about it that he can't wait to tell other people who suffer from the same illness where to find the cure. If this happened to you, to keep that knowledge to yourself would be one of the most selfish things you could do.

Besides the issue of feeling unprepared or being afraid, another objection to evangelism I hear is that the people at our office or in our circle of friends and acquaintances aren't really interested in hearing about Jesus.

## EVERY PERSON HAS FOUR NEEDS THAT ONLY JESUS CAN MEET

Well, I beg to differ. Yes, they may not want to be pinned to the wall with a Bible under their nose, but that's not really New Testament evangelism anyway. And people are incredibly interested in something that will fill the void in their hearts. No matter how "together" and happy people may look externally, and no matter whether they live in a flophouse or a penthouse, all people have four basic, inescapable needs on the inside that can be met only by Jesus Christ. They just need someone to introduce them to Him.

### Every Person Is Spiritually Empty

There is, as we have heard many times, a God-shaped vacuum in every human heart—a spiritual niche created by God for His presence and His presence alone.

Therefore, the fact is that every person who has ever been born is on a spiritual search, whether they realize it or have admitted it or not.

### Every Person Is Lonely Without God

We hear psychologists talk about "cosmic loneliness." This is the uneasy sense a person has that he is alone in the universe. The next time you're in your marketplace and it is crowded with people, look around you. You are looking into the faces of many lonely people.

They may be surrounded by friends and family. They may be at the very top of their field. But there is a basic spiritual loneliness in the human heart. We are born separated from God, which creates an alienation and feeling of loneliness that no amount of parties and no crowd of people can fill. God made us for a relationship with Him through Jesus Christ.

### Every Person Has Sinned and Is In Need of Forgiveness

Every person is guilty of sin and needs God's forgiveness. "All have sinned and fall short of the glory of God" (Romans 3:23) is part of the ABCs of the gospel. People realize deep down that they have failed to live up to their own standards, much less to the standards of God.

Many people try to suppress their guilt or blur it with alcohol or drugs or pleasure of all kinds, but everyone has a sense of guilt because of sin. They would welcome the news that they can be totally forgiven and have every stain removed. But many people don't know that such forgiveness is available to them. They also don't realize that their sin has extreme consequences—separation from God forever in hell.

I heard a pastor tell a group of pastors one time, "We don't really need to say much about sin in the pulpit because people already know they're sinners."

That's dubious advice at best, but even granting the fact that people already know they are sinners doesn't excuse us from dealing with sin. The problem in this generation is that instead of at least being embarrassed about their sin as people used to be, people today celebrate it! They go on television and talk about it. Their attitude is, "So I'm a sinner. Big deal. Everybody does it."

Well, sin *is* a big deal because it carries big-time consequences. People need to know that "the wages of sin is death" (Romans 6:23). We need to help people understand that sin and the guilt they feel are not only real, but that sin is a cancer that will ultimately destroy both body and soul in hell.

### Every Person Is Afraid to Die

Nobody likes to talk about the "D" word. Even when people die, we say, "He passed away," "She went to her reward," or something similar. But the fact is that "it is appointed for men to die once" (Hebrews 9:27).

I was with a group of men one day when this one guy began expounding on his religion, which was not a living faith in Christ. He started to tell us, "If I die, this is what's going to happen."

I just had to speak up. "Wait a minute," I said to him. "It's not *if* you die; it's *when* you die," because all of us have a date with death unless Christ returns in our lifetime. I'm looking forward to His return, but the truth is that death is on our calendar.

For people who don't know Christ, there is a natural fear of death. People want to know, "What comes after death?" They have an innate sense that this life is not all there is because the Scripture says God has "put eternity" in the heart of man (Ecclesiastes 3:11). God made us immortal, eternal souls, and when He breathed into us the breath of life, we became eternal beings with an awareness of eternity in our hearts.

Fear of death is a human need that drives people to seek answers to this life and the life beyond, and it can be a powerful ally in our evangelism. We don't have to scare people into heaven—although if that's the only way some people will ever get there, then I'm for it!

When they put their heads on their pillows at night, many people think about death and what lies ahead of them. The good news is that Jesus can "release those who through fear of death were all their lifetime subject to bondage" (Hebrews 2:15).

So people are empty and lonely and guilty and afraid to die— and that includes people at your place of work and in the other areas of your marketplace. The best mission field on earth for you to touch is not necessarily somewhere on the opposite side of the world, but right there in your office or neighborhood. Every person you touch in the marketplace is a prospect for new life in Christ.

## THERE ARE FOUR GREAT GIFTS YOU CAN SHARE WITH OTHERS

We not only need to be convinced that lost people need and want to know about Christ. We also need to know what to share with them. The Bible calls salvation "the gift of God . . . eternal life in Christ Jesus our Lord" (Romans 6:23). So let me give you four powerful gifts you can share with the people around you who don't know Jesus Christ.

### You Can Share with Lost People the Testimony of a Changed Life

If you have been set free from your sin by faith in Christ—if you have been cured of the fatal disease of sin—then you have something very powerful to share with others.

John 9 tells the story of a man born blind who was healed by Jesus. I encourage you to read the chapter. This was the happiest day of this poor guy's life, and the religious leaders called him on the carpet and gave him a hard time because he could see! They were angry when he told them that Jesus healed him, because they were Jesus' enemies and wanted to destroy Him.

The formerly blind man couldn't answer all their questions because he wasn't even sure himself who Jesus was. But he had a testimony of a changed life, so when they kept pressing him he finally said in exasperation, "One thing I know: that though I was blind, now I see" (John 9:25).

Brother, you don't have to have all the answers or know all the arguments. Don't wait until you can answer every question that someone may ask you. A lot of men hesitate to share their faith because they're afraid somebody is going to ask something they can't deal with.

As men we tend to have a lot of pride and don't want to embarrass ourselves or embarrass the Lord, so we just clam up rather than take the risk that someone is going to put us on the spot. We need to have the spirit of the blind man in John 9: "Look, I can't answer all your questions, but I know what happened to me. I once was blind, but now I can see. I once was lost, but now I'm found. I have been delivered and changed by Jesus Christ."

Jesus said, "Let your light so shine before men, that they may see your good works and glorify your Father in heaven" (Matthew

5:16). That's what we're talking about. Don't ever forget that a man with a testimony is never at the mercy of a man with an argument!

I'm not saying we shouldn't learn how to defend our faith or know the basics of Christian doctrine. Peter wrote, "Sanctify the Lord God in your hearts, and always be ready to give a defense to everyone who asks you a reason for the hope that is in you, with meekness and fear" (1 Peter 3:15). The Greek word translated "defense" is the basis of our word "apologetics," which means a reasoned defense of the faith.

But if we wait until we've got all the answers, then most of us will never get around to being a witness for Christ. You can begin tomorrow telling others what Christ has done for you.

This is what the apostle Paul did. Paul was a trained Pharisee and rabbi who was probably the most brilliant man of his day. He could have overwhelmed people with arguments. But when Paul gave his testimony before King Agrippa in Acts 26, his basic argument was, "This is what happened to me. This is how Christ changed my life."

Your testimony may not be dramatic or filled with gory details, but if Christ has taken you from death to life, you have something incredible to share!

I was saved as a child. I wasn't on anybody's most wanted list. I didn't have a terrible life to repent of. But I knew that I was a sinner and I knew that I needed a Savior. My testimony is one of God's faithfulness through the years.

Can you tell someone what Jesus has done for you? Sure, you can! People want to know your experience—especially if they see the reality of Christ in your life. This is one thing that makes marketplace evangelism so effective. People who work with us and know us can see the change.

You can begin a witness by asking permission: "Would you mind if I tell you what God has done in my life?" That opens an opportunity to share your faith without getting into people's faces. Instead, you get into their hearts.

## *You Can Share with Lost People a Confident Faith*

We also have a confident faith to share with others. We need boldness in our witness. Someone once asked a guy if he believed what a Christian friend had been sharing with him. "Well," he answered, "I'm not sure if I believe it, but he sure does!" We owe it to people to be confident of God's power at work in us to be effective in our witness.

You don't have to shake in your boots at the thought of witnessing to a lost person. If you know Jesus, you have something to be confident about. I like the way the New International Version states it: "Such confidence as this is ours through Christ before God. Not that we are competent in ourselves to claim anything for ourselves, but our competence comes from God" (2 Corinthians 3:4-5). We can be both confident and competent in the power of the Holy Spirit.

When Jesus commissioned His followers to go into all the world, He said, "You shall receive power when the Holy Spirit has come upon you; and you shall be witnesses to Me" (Acts 1:8). We have a confident faith we can share with others because God has promised that the Holy Spirit will partner with us in our evangelism. All we have to do is be obedient to our commission. The Holy Spirit will enable and empower us as we share the message of Christ.

God gets excited, if you will, when He sees us obeying Him. The Holy Spirit says, "Here is a man who is doing what he has been called to do. I will empower his witness!"

I love the way Bill Bright defined witnessing: "Witnessing is simply sharing Jesus Christ in the power of the Holy Spirit, and leaving the results to God." Doesn't it give you confidence to know that you are not responsible for the results of your witness?

That is freeing to me, because it means I don't have to manipulate or badger people. I can be confident that God will plant the seed of His Word in the hearts of the unsaved people I witness to.

We can confidently tell people that if they will come to Christ, confess their sins, and believe on Him as their Savior, they can be saved. That's a confident faith.

### You Can Share with Lost People a Compassionate Heart

A third incredible gift you have to share with others is a compassionate heart. We are going to get excited about sharing our faith when God begins to burden our hearts for our lost family members and friends.

Paul is our example again. He said in Romans 9:2-4, "I have great sorrow and continual grief in my heart. For I could wish that I myself were accursed from Christ for my brethren, my countrymen according to the flesh, who are Israelites."

Paul's compassion for his Jewish brothers and sisters was so great that he would have done anything to see them come to Christ. If you really care about people, it will show in every word you say to them. It's an old saying, but it's true: people don't care how much we know until they know how much we care. When the love of Christ is evident in our hearts, people will respond to that love.

Alexander McLaren, a great pastor of an earlier day, said, "You tell me the depth of a Christian's compassion, and I will tell you the measure of his usefulness." If you want to be a man of God whom He can use, then ask Him to give you an unquenchable love and burden for people in your marketplace who are lost and heading to a Christless eternity.

Let's be honest. One reason we don't share our faith with others more often is that we just don't care. I say that because if we truly cared about people who don't know Jesus, and believed that they were on their way to life without God forever, we could not be silent.

We need to ask God to give us a burden for souls. This should be a part of your daily prayer life: "Lord, give me a burden for people. Make me sensitive to those who don't know Jesus. Open my eyes, Lord, that I can see people who need You."

Many times we walk right past opportunities to share our faith.

I remember one occasion when I was playing golf with several other men. We were guests of a wonderful man who has an extreme compassion for lost people, and we had stopped to pray before we started playing. By the time we got to the ninth hole, this man had engaged one of our caddies in conversation, shared his faith, and this young man prayed to receive Christ.

Where was Pastor Jack while this was happening? I have to confess, I hadn't even thought about sharing my faith with that caddie. I was having a full-time job just trying to hit the ball. But while I was addressing the ball, my friend was addressing a young man who needed Jesus. I learned a lesson that day that I will never forget.

If you want to have a heart of compassion, be sensitive to people around you, build relationships, and start seeing people as God sees them. Godly compassion isn't some mysterious feeling that just drops out of the sky on you one day. It is the result of cultivating a caring heart for lost people.

### You Can Share with Lost People a Compelling Message

Here's the fourth gift you have to share with people around you who need to know Jesus. The gospel is a compelling message with a built-in invitation and urgency to it. Paul wrote, "We are ambassadors for Christ, as though God were *pleading* through us: we *implore* you on Christ's behalf, be reconciled to God" (2 Corinthians 5:20, emphasis added).

The gospel is compelling when lost people hear it presented in the power of the Holy Spirit and the love of Christ. It also needs to be compelling to us, the most important thing we have to tell anyone. Again, we turn to Paul: "For I am not ashamed of the gospel of Christ, for it is the power of God to salvation for everyone who believes" (Romans 1:16).

The word *power* here is *dunamis*—dynamic, explosive power. Don't underestimate the power of the gospel. You have a message that is powerful and persuasive. You don't have to take away from it or add to it. Just clearly share it.

Until we have shared the gospel, we have not completed our

mission. Our personal testimony can be powerful, but it needs to be followed with the gospel and what the person we are talking to needs to believe. Paul summarized the gospel: "I declare to you the gospel. . . . that Christ died for our sins according to the Scriptures, and that He was buried, and that He rose again the third day according to the Scriptures" (1 Corinthians 15:1, 3-4).

The gospel is compelling, and it needs to be told in a confident, compelling way. A story was told about a young man who was witnessing to a friend one day for whom he had a deep burden. The Christian shared the gospel with his lost friend, but the friend rejected it.

All of a sudden, this Christian young man began to cry. When his friend asked him what was wrong, he said, "I'm sorry, man. I must not have done a very good job of presenting the gospel to you, or you would have believed it."

His friend was so taken aback by this man's apology that he asked him to try again, and this time he "got it" and came to faith in Christ!

I pray that we will have this same sense of compulsion about the gospel. If your office building were on fire and your coworkers were in peril of their lives, you would not be afraid to tell them about the fire, or casually whisper it under your breath. You would shout the news at the top of your lungs, especially if you knew a safe way out of the building. And if a friend laughed at you and said he didn't believe you, you'd grab him by the arm and say, "You've got to listen to me! You've got to get out of here now!"

May God give us that kind of fire in our hearts, because people in our marketplace are in eternal peril without Christ. My prayer is that you will be a faithful man of God in your witness for Him.

## A FINAL WORD

My brother in Christ, I pray that my passion and conviction—and my confidence that we can be men of God—has come through in these pages. I am convinced there is not one truth or challenge in this book that cannot be put into practice in our lives by the power of the Holy Spirit who lives within us.

In fact, I believe that if anything, the church of Jesus Christ has been guilty of *under*-challenging men to step up and take spiritual leadership. So I never apologize for strongly calling men to be men of God. Anything less than that is not worthy of our best commitment! With that in mind, let me leave you with a final word of challenge, taken from the writings of my greatest hero in the faith, the apostle Paul.

In the book of Ephesians, Paul called us as believers to live for eternity. That's really what it's all about. Here are four things we need to do *now* as men of God to live lives that will count both for time and for eternity:

### It's Time to Look Up

Dr. W. A. Criswell, the late, great pastor of First Baptist Church of Dallas, used to challenge us, "Look up, brothers!"

In Ephesians 1:3 we're told, "Blessed be the God and Father of our Lord Jesus Christ, who has blessed us with every spiritual blessing in the heavenly places in Christ." Every abundant provision of God and resource for the task at hand is already given to us. We are amazingly and abundantly blessed.

This verse is written in a Greek tense which indicates that God's act of blessing us has already happened and is still in effect. We have been blessed, we are blessed, and we will be blessed forevermore. Let's not forget that our hope and strength come from heaven.

### It's Time to Step Up

As men of God, we must "walk worthy of the calling with which [we] were called" (Ephesians 4:1). We're also told to "walk in love" and "walk circumspectly," or carefully (5:2, 15).

This means not only watching our step in terms of steering clear of evil. The far greater challenge for us is to walk intentionally, that is, to set our feet and our hearts toward serving the Lord in the home, the church, and the marketplace.

None of my baseball coaches ever told me, "Now remember, when you're rounding first, make sure you don't trip over the right-fielder." Why? Because the right-fielder is not in the path to second base. All I needed to do was run like crazy to second base with my eyes straight ahead. Let's step it up for the Lord Jesus.

## It's Time to Wise Up

This is the challenge of Ephesians 5:17-18: "Therefore do not be unwise, but understand what the will of the Lord is. And do not be drunk with wine, in which is dissipation; but be filled with the Spirit."

We're to walk in wisdom because we are in a cultural war like none we've ever seen before, and things are not going well for the good guys! We are part of a struggle that will define America and the world for generations to come. Jesus taught us to be "wise as serpents and harmless as doves" (Matthew 10:16).

This means to think biblically and live truthfully—to live distinctively different Christian lives in this culture. To wise up is to live in the power of God's Spirit and express the life and the love of Jesus in the culture.

## It's Time to Gear Up

Guys love hardware, so this should be a piece of cake! We're in a battle not with other people, "but against principalities, against powers, against the rulers of the darkness of this age, against spiritual hosts of wickedness in the heavenly places" (Ephesians 6:12).

We are at a tremendous advantage in this war. We know who the enemy is and where he is. We know his strategy and his movements. We even know the outcome of the battle—but we still need to put on the armor of God (Ephesians 6:13-18) and stand ready for the fight. We must not relent, retreat, flinch, or fail. God's Kingdom is forever, and His Word will stand forever (Isaiah 40:8)! We win, brother! God bless you as you determine to be a man of God.

# GENERAL INDEX

Graham, Tom (author's father), 110, 146, 170, 192

Ham, Mordecai, 183-184
Havner, Vance, 22
Holy Spirit, the, 30, 135
Hunt, William Holman, 30

Iraq, conflict in, 56, 149
Isaac, 145

Jacob, 145, 195
James, 25
Jeremiah, David, 137
Jesus Christ: intimacy of His presence in our lives, 28-29; as a personal Lord, 188; as a physical Lord, 187-188; as the preeminent Lord, 187; sharing, 186. *See also* Jesus Christ, need for
Jesus Christ, need for, 201; and fear of death, 202-203; and loneliness without God, 201-202; and sin, 202; and spiritual emptiness, 201
Job, 149
John, 25
Jude, 178

Keil, James, 56-57
Kennedy, John F., 108
Kennedy, John, Jr., 109
Kennedy, Rose, 109
Kimball, Edward, 182, 184
*koinonia*, 61

Lasorda, Tommy, 190-191
Lazarus, 193

Leman, Kevin, 124
*Light of the World*, 30
Lincoln, Abraham, 132
Lombardi, Vince, 181
love, types of: *agape*, 130; *eros*, 130; *phileo*, 130
Luther, Martin, 157
Lyndon B. Johnson Freeway, 71

manhood: and gender roles, 20-21; and lifestyle choices, 49-51; "macho" men, 21; "sensitive" men, 21. *See also* men, as light of the world; men, as salt of the earth
marriage, 118, 119-120. *See also* wives, love for
Martha, 193
Marx, Groucho, 142
Mary of Bethany, 193
Matthew, 24-25
Maxwell, John, 171
McLaren, Alexander, 207
Melchizedek, 113
men, as light of the world, 55; compelling light, 57; consistent light, 56-57; conspicuous light, 55-56; consuming light, 57-58
men, as salt of the earth, 51-52; containing our salt, 54-55; diluting our salt, 54; and the salt of witness in our culture, 52-54
mentoring, 169-171; accomplishments of, 182-184. *See also* mentoring, need for; mentoring others
mentoring, need for, 171; for confronting us, 172-173; for

# SCRIPTURE INDEX

# STUDY GUIDE

## HOW TO USE THIS STUDY GUIDE

Welcome to this interactive study guide for *A Man of God*. If you have taken seriously the challenges in the opening pages, you are ready to reflect personally on the biblical principles in these chapters. You may even be ready to meet with other men and hold each other accountable as men of God. This guide has been designed to help both of those purposes: individual reflection and group study.

You can use this guide in two ways and in two settings. The book is divided into four major parts and twelve chapters. This guide has been built to facilitate a study based either on the parts (which would involve a four-session study) or on the chapters (which would take up to twelve or more sessions to accomplish). You might also decide to use the chapter lessons as you work through the book and then use the part sessions to review and keep the big picture in mind. These approaches can be used individually and in a group. Consider doing both. As you will learn through this book, you may have to be a man of God alone from time to time, but you will not become or remain a man of God without the company of other men of God. Share this experience with other men.

Each of the sessions has the same structure: *Location*, *Clues*, and *Direction*. The *Location* questions will help you track your personal condition in relation to the message of the book. You need to know where you are before you take the next step. The *Clues* questions will help you break down the chapter into the key components. Each chapter's *Clues* section will also include a list of Scripture passages from the book. The *Direction* questions will help you identify personal application decisions and actions you can take based on what you are discovering.

## 4 SAKES PRAYER

In the Introduction, a prayer is offered for the men who will read this book. Consider yourself having been prayed for as well as having been given a valuable prayer you can use. Your study of this book and the Book behind it will help this prayer come true in your life:

*For the sake of the Kingdom,*
*For the sake of my family,*
*For the sake of God's church,*
*And for the sake of our nation,*
*I will become a man of God.*

# Introductory Session

Note: You can use this session as a warm-up for a group that is meeting for the first time to discuss *A Man of God*. Hopefully, these questions and the discussion that occurs will encourage those who have not begun to read the book to do so before the next session.

## Location

1. What would it be like to receive a job reference or recommendation from Chuck Norris?

2. As you begin this study, briefly jot below your present understanding of what it means to be a man of God.

3. How would you describe your main reason for reading/studying this book?

## Clues

4. In his Foreword, Chuck Norris talks about his experiences in church. How does church fit in your life right now?

5. In the Introduction, we considered that the key to a new vitality in the church will be "because men became godly and began living their faith with passion and integrity" (p. 13). What men, if any, do you know who fit that description?

6. Read the following statement about God's interest in men who will live for Him: "The eyes of the Lord run to and from throughout the whole earth, to show Himself strong on behalf of those whose heart is loyal to Him" (2 Chronicles 16:9). What does "loyal heart" mean to you?

## Direction

7. What would it take for you to commit to see this study through to the end?

8. Tell at least one other person that you're doing this study and ask that person to check on your progress in the next few weeks. Whom will you tell?

9. Read through the 4 Sakes Prayer found in the book (p. 13) or in the instructions at the beginning of this guide.

# PART ONE SESSION
# A MAN OF GOD AND HIS MASTER

## LOCATION

1. In your work experiences, who has been the best boss you ever worked for? Why?

2. When people use the term "Master" to describe Jesus, to what do you think they are referring?

3. What would it be like to work in a place where Jesus is boss?

## CLUES

4. Chapter 1 defines *Maximum Discipleship*. What is it, and what can you expect to experience if you view your relationship with Jesus Christ in that way?

5. Chapter 2 lays out the demands and details of following Jesus as Master. What would it take, and what do you expect would happen if you really treated Jesus as Master of your life?

6. What are the most obvious areas in which your lifestyle mirrors or fails to mirror the Maximum Discipleship lifestyle explained in chapter 3?

## DIRECTION

7. How did you respond to the challenge of chapter 1 to "decide today to go all out for Christ"? What, if anything, is holding you back?

8. In what ways have you or haven't you let Jesus take charge of your life?

9. Based on chapter 3, how would you describe the role of the church of Jesus Christ in shaping your lifestyle? What, if any, changes do you need to make in that relationship?

## Lesson One
# A Commitment to Maximum Discipleship

### Location

1. Who's the best living example to represent the meaning of *commitment*? Why?

2. How did you react to the observation about watching Roger Clemens at the World Series in 2003 (see pp. 19-20)?

3. Identify three current commitments in your life: one long-term, one short-term, and one open-ended commitment.

### Clues

*Key Scriptures:* 2 Chronicles 16:9; Matthew 4:18-22; 6:33; 10:25; 25:21; Mark 8:34; Luke 5:27; John 15:1-17; Philippians 1:21; 3:13-14; Revelation 3:15-16

4. What's the difference between *burning* out and *maxing* out for Christ (see p. 21)?

5. What does each of the following verses tell you about being God's man?

    2 Chronicles 16:9

    Philippians 1:21

    Matthew 6:33

6. What warnings did we consider about "cruise control" and "microwave" spiritual lives (see pp. 23-24)?

### Direction

7. In what way do we need to change our minds about the Christian life (p. 24)? To what degree does your mind need changing?

8. Three powerful changes will result when we "follow Jesus in all-out, maximum commitment" (pp. 25-29). Describe each briefly:

1. You will . . .

2. You will . . .

3. You will . . .

9. What examples are given on pages 29-30 to clarify the difficulties we face in going "all out for Christ"? How well does this describe the challenge for you? What's the present status of your relationship with Christ?

LESSON TWO
# WHAT IT MEANS TO FOLLOW THE MASTER

## LOCATION

1. Whether it's a two-week fishing trip into the wilderness of Canada or a multi-stop business trip, what have you discovered are the most important preparation steps to take before you leave home?

2. This chapter begins with an honest inquiry into whether the church "has always been straightforward with Christians about what it costs to be Jesus' disciple" (p. 33). How do you react to that statement?

3. What are your passions?

## CLUES

*Key Scriptures:* Matthew 4:18-22; 10:25; 14:13-21; 22:39; 26:56; Mark 2:14; Luke 9:23-24; 14:16-35; John 2:25; 21:1-22; Romans 12:3; 1 Corinthians 11:31; 15:31; Galatians 2:20; Philippians 1:20; Hebrews 12:1

4. Reflect and respond to this statement and these questions: "Remember, the issue is not your perfection, but your direction. Are you moving toward Christian maturity, or away from it? Maybe a better question would be, Are you a fully *developing* follower of Jesus Christ? We may not be perfectly devoted, but we can be developing—growing in the love and grace of Jesus Christ. Is the desire of your heart that Jesus be the Master of your life?" (p. 34).

5. Briefly describe the two passions that a man needs in order to be Jesus' disciple (pp. 34-37).

6. What are the three primary demands that men should "count" or "take into account" before deciding to max out for Jesus (pp. 37-41)?

    1. We must . . .

    2. We must . . .

    3. We must . . .

## DIRECTION

7. Using the explanations given on pages 42-44, where would you place yourself on the following continuum? Why?

Clueless    ⟶    Curious    ⟶    Convinced    ⟶    Committed
about Jesus           about Jesus         about Jesus         to Jesus

8. On page 45 we read, "What will it take for us to go from being merely curious or convinced about Jesus to being totally committed to Him?" Describe each of these steps and what you have done about them to this point:

1. Being Committed to Jesus Starts with *Denying Yourself.*

2. Being Committed to Jesus Means *Taking Up Your Cross.*

3. Being Committed to Jesus Means *Following Him.*

9. How did you respond to the final question of this chapter: "Are you ready for the challenge of letting the Master take charge?" Why or why not?

LESSON THREE

# THE IMPORTANCE OF A MAN'S LIFESTYLE

## LOCATION

1. Describe a situation in which you identified someone as, or you yourself were identified as a follower of Jesus based on behavior and responses. What gave them or you away?

2. Based on what you've read in *A Man of God*, respond to the Winston Churchill quote: "To each there comes in their lifetime a special moment when they are figuratively tapped on the shoulder and offered the chance to do a very special thing, unique to them and fitted to their talents. What a tragedy if that moment finds them unprepared and unqualified for that which could have been their finest hour" (p. 50).

## CLUES

*Key Scriptures:* Matthew 5:13-16; 6:33; 24:21; John 8:12; 14:15; Romans 1:16; 1 Corinthians 14:24-25; 2 Corinthians 4:6; Ephesians 4:12-16; 2 Thessalonians 2:7; 2 Timothy 3:13; Hebrews 2:11; 10:24-25; 13:7,13,17; 1 Peter 2:9; 1 John 1:3

3. Read Matthew 5:13-16. Based on those verses, what does it mean to say, "If we're going to make a difference, then we must be different" (p. 51)?

4. Complete and describe what is meant by each of the following statements (pp. 52-54):

A. The Salt of Our Witness Should . . .

B. The Salt of Our Witness Should . . .

C. The Salt of Our Witness Should . . .

5. What two warnings does the book include regarding the condition of the salt (p. 54)? How would you illustrate these from your own observations?

6. Identify four qualities of light that must characterize our lives as followers of Jesus (pp. 55-58):

1. We are to shine a _____ light.

2. We are to shine a _____ light.

3. We are to shine a _____ light.

4. We are to shine a _____ light.

Which do you find most challenging? Why?

## DIRECTION

7. The chapter ends with a strong case for the importance of the church as a primary influence and outlet in the life of a man of God. There are seven reasons: We should be committed to the church of Jesus Christ . . .

> . . . out of loving obedience.
> . . . to experience fellowship.
> . . . for spiritual leadership (guidance).
> . . . because of our identity.
> . . . out of loyalty.
> . . . as our place of ministry.
> . . . because of our witness.

Which one of these do you find most compelling in your life? Why?

8. What difference would it make to you and to your church if you withdrew completely from that church?

9. What are the main ways in which you now participate in your local church? Which of these could be increased? How could you deepen your participation in at least one specific area?

# PART TWO SESSION
# A MAN OF GOD
# AND HIS INTEGRITY

## LOCATION

1. Think about two or three men who have been heroes for you. In what ways has their integrity been a factor in causing your admiration?

2. What does the word *integrity* mean to you?

3. What can a person do to change or improve his or her integrity?

## CLUES

4. Men today are often criticized for being either indecisive or foolishly decisive. How might chapter 4 help you improve your record for "taking it" when you come to a fork in the road?

5. List the five "narrow road" decisions described in chapter 4 (pp. 76-78) in the order of priority they occupy in your life right now. Then briefly describe your reasons for ordering them this way.

    1.

    2.

    3.

    4.

    5.

6. Why have we devoted so much space in chapters 4 and 5 to the issue of moral purity? In what ways does P-U-R-E (p. 88) help you?

7. What were your first responses as you read through the five points under "We Need to Get Our Thinking Straight About the Money God Entrusts to Us" (p. 102)?

## DIRECTION

8. How do you act differently depending on whether you think someone, or no one, is watching?

9. What would you like your children and friends to remember about your integrity at your memorial service?

## Lesson Four
# Facing a Fork in the Road

### Location

1. Think about the five most difficult decisions you've ever had to make. Describe one of those decisions.

2. Who is a reliable mentor for you in the area of decision making?

3. What is the first question you ask when you come to a "fork in the road"?

### Clues

*Key Scriptures:* 1 Samuel 12:23; 2 Samuel 11; Psalm 119:9; Proverbs 23:7; Ecclesiastes 2:1-11; Daniel 1:8; Matthew 5:9; 7:13-14; Mark 8:34-37; Luke 16:19-31; Acts 13:22; Romans 13:14; 1 Corinthians 3:13; 10:12; Philippians 4:8, 13; 1 Thessalonians 5:22; 2 Timothy 2:22; Hebrews 12:15-16; 1 John 1:9

4. What is the broad and easy road, and why does it lead to so many problems?

5. Describe the two primary benefits of the narrow road.

6. Review Patrick Morley's "exercise" (top of p. 75). How did you answer the questions?

### Direction

7. Identify each of the five integrity decisions that will measure your pace on the narrow road with Christ (see pp. 76-78). Then put a plus sign next to those you have already made.

    1. Decide you will be . . .

    2. Decide you will be . . .

    3. Decide you will be . . .

    4. Decide you will be . . .

    5. Decide you will be . . .

8. There are ten moral decisions related to the single area of sexual purity. List them below and mark those for which you need greater understanding and consistency.

1. Accept your . . .

2. Affirm that you . . .

3. Aim to be . . .

4. Abandon all . . .

5. Avoid the . . .

6. Abstain from . . .

7. Abide in . . .

8. Arm yourself with . . .

9. Affirm the . . .

10. Remember that you . . .

9. Which of the first four decisions in question 7 do you think would help you the most in keeping the fifth decision to be morally pure? To what degree have you kept that decision?

## LESSON FIVE
# A CALL TO MORAL PURITY

## LOCATION

1. Which of the ten aspects of sexual purity in the last lesson present an immediate challenge to you?

2. How do you respond to the statement on page 85, "I think you will agree with me that it is impossible to be a man of God without making a commitment to faithfulness and purity in refraining from sexual sin, both in our minds and in our bodies"?

3. If someone spotted you reading this book and asked you about the title, what would you say was the purpose of the book?

## CLUES

*Key Scriptures:* Numbers 32:23; Psalm 119:11; Nahum 1:3; Matthew 22:37; Romans 12:1; 13:12-14; 2 Corinthians 6:14-18; 7:1; Galatians 5:16; 1 Peter 1:15-16; 5:8

4. Why is this chapter titled "A Call to Moral Purity" rather than "A Call to Avoid Sexual Immorality"?

5. Briefly explain each of the action words and phrases that make up the acronym P-U-R-E:

    Prepare

    Undo

    Remember

    Engage

6. What explanation is given for the warning not to set yourself up for moral failure (pp. 92-94)?

## DIRECTION

7. Each of the items in the acronym P-U-R-E represents an action to take. The fourth action, *Engage,* is described as the "replacement principle" (p. 96). What does that mean?

8. List below each of the "engagement" spiritual activities described on pages 96-97. Note how you are doing with each of those areas.

A.

B.

C.

D.

9. Which one of those areas will get special attention from you this week?

LESSON SIX

# A MAN AND HIS MONEY

## LOCATION

1. What experiences in your life parallel the story about the young builder at the beginning of this chapter (pp. 99-100)?

2. What is your understanding of the concept of stewardship? (If this is a new idea for you, see p. 101.)

3. What public figure would you use to illustrate effective stewardship? Why?

## CLUES

*Key Scriptures:* Genesis 14:20; Exodus 20:15; 22:1; Leviticus 19:11; Deuteronomy 8:18; 23:19; Joshua 1:8; Psalms 1:3; 24:1; 37:21; Proverbs 3:5-6, 9; 6:6-8; 11:1; 13:11; 21:20; Ecclesiastes 5:19; Jeremiah 22:13; Ezekiel 46:16; Haggai 2:8; Malachi 3:8; Matthew 6:21; 23:23; Luke 12:48; 16; Romans 13:8; 1 Corinthians 4:7; 16:2; 2 Corinthians 9:7; Ephesians 1:3; 2 Thessalonians 3:10; 1 Timothy 6:6-7; James 5:4; 3 John 2

4. Summarize the five "biblical ways to think about the money God gives us as His stewards or managers."

5. What are some of the ways that we can *wrongfully* gain money (pp. 105-111)?

How can we gain money *rightfully?*

6. Why and how should we "guard" the money we have (pp. 111-112)?

7. How does "giving" or "tithing" fit into your understanding of money management?

## DIRECTION

8. If you were to become convinced that "God cares about what we do with the other nine-tenths" beyond the tithe, in what ways, if any, would that affect your lifestyle?

9. When have you practiced and experienced "cheerful giving"?

10. How has your view of stewardship been shaped or sharpened as a result of this lesson/chapter?

## PART THREE SESSION
# A MAN OF GOD AND HIS FAMILY

### LOCATION

1. What men have been significant examples for you regarding the roles of father and husband?

2. If you could woo and marry your wife again, what aspects of your relationship development would you improve?

3. What are your top three priorities as a father?

### CLUES

4. After reading chapter 7, what would you say are the primary aspects of living with your lady "in an understanding way"? What is your greatest personal challenge in that relationship?

5. Based on chapter 8, complete the following lists of priorities:

A. Three ways in which I can protect my family.

1.

2.

3.

B. Three ways in which I can bless my family.

1.

2.

3.

6. What does it mean to be living a legacy for children?

## DIRECTION

7. One of the subtitles in chapter 7 is the challenge adapted from 1 Peter 3:7 to live with our wives in an understanding way. Based on what you've read, what are you doing in a specific area of your marriage to live with your wife "in an understanding way"?

8. What changes do you need to make to be better able to protect and bless your family?

9. How have your prayers for your family changed as a result of reading the chapter about legacy?

LESSON SEVEN
# LOVING THE LADY IN YOUR LIFE

## LOCATION

1. Where did you meet your wife and where did you ask her to marry you?

2. Describe one of the qualities of your wife that strongly influenced you to decide, "I'm going to ask her to marry me."

3. Think for a moment about the growth process of an oak, from acorn to mighty tree. Every year's growth adds a ring to the tree. Bear in mind also the possible dangers of lightning strikes, forest fires, and pests of different kinds. What's the condition of the "oak" that represents your marriage?

## CLUES

*Key Scriptures:* Genesis 2:24; Matthew 8:14-15; John 10:29; Romans 8:35-39; 1 Corinthians 9:5; Ephesians 5:22-33; Philippians 2:1-8; Hebrews 12:2; 1 Peter 3:7; 2 Peter 3:18

4. Based on Ephesians 5:25, in what ways is *loving* your wife just as much a challenge for *you* as the command to *submit* to you is a challenge for your wife (see p. 119)?

5. At this point in your marriage, which of the nine things "Women Want and Need" (pp. 120-125) do you think you're doing a pretty good job providing?

6. Think about the nine key relational needs our wives have that are important for us to understand. The tenth "need" (p. 126) turns out to be a need that *we husbands* have. How does your desire for a healthy relationship with God affect the way you carry out your role as a husband?

7. On pages 126-135, we read about the six aspects of loving our wives as Christ loves the church. Briefly describe each aspect ("I must . . .") and then give yourself a current grade (A, B, C, D, F) for each of them:

*We must love our wives selflessly*—Current grade: _____
I must . . .

*We must love our wives sacrificially*—Current grade: _____
I must . . .

*We must love our wives sanctifyingly*—Current grade: _____
I must . . .

*We must love our wives satisfyingly*—Current grade: _____
I must . . .

*We must love our wives supremely*—Current grade: _____
I must . . .

*We must love our wives steadfastly*—Current grade: _____
I must . . .

## DIRECTION

8. There are nine things "Women Want and Need" (plus a tenth that is personal to you—p. 126). Write out these nine needs on a separate piece of paper and give them to your wife, asking her to help you by prioritizing them. Ask her to describe what each of the underlined words means to her.

Nine things "Women Want and Need":

1. Women Want and Need *Togetherness*
2. Women Want and Need *Tenderness*
3. Women Want and Need *Empathy*
4. Women Want and Need *Spiritual Encouragement*
5. Women Want and Need *Appreciation*
6. Women Want and Need *Time*
7. Women Want and Need *Conversation*
8. Women Want and Need *Praise*
9. Women Want and Need *Consideration*

Write out your wife's prioritized list of wants and needs. Refer to this list as a guide to living with your wife in an understanding way:

1. I Want and Need . . .
2. I Want and Need . . .
3. I Want and Need . . .
4. I Want and Need . . .
5. I Want and Need . . .
6. I Want and Need . . .
7. I Want and Need . . .
8. I Want and Need . . .
9. I Want and Need . . .

9. Describe for future reference your wife's responses to this assignment, what you learned about her (and your relationship with her), and two or three decisions you have made about "loving the lady in your life."

## Lesson Eight
# Protecting and Blessing Your Family

### Location

1. What have been some of the strongest positive and negative lasting effects on your life from the family of your youth?

2. These days, what do you find most enjoyable about being a father?

3. What's one area of your relationship with your children that you'd like to improve?

### Clues

*Key Scriptures:* Genesis 27; 49; Job 1:5; 23:12; Psalms 58:3; 101:3; 127:3; Proverbs 1:7, 8-19; 2:10-15; 4:11, 23; 13:20; 14:26, 27; 20:7; 22:15; 23:7; Matthew 6:9-13; Luke 22:42; Romans 8:29; 1 Corinthians 15:33; 2 Corinthians 2:14; Galatians 6:7; Ephesians 4:13-16; 6:10-18; 1 Thessalonians 4:3; 5:17

4. What "gifts" of lasting and eternal value that you can give to your children are described in this chapter?

5. Which of these "gifts" are you already giving and which ones need to be a greater priority in your home?

6. There are nine qualities that should be part of the way we pray for our children (pp. 147-151). List and make short comments on each one:

    1.

    2.

    3.

    4.

    5.

    6.

    7.

8.

9.

## DIRECTION

7. On page 144, we read about the importance of having fun as a dad. How would your children rate you according to this statement: "My dad knows how to have fun"?

8. Note the fatherly exercise in the middle of page 143. It has a personal part and a part you will do with your kids. When will you carry out this exercise?

9. The next chapter deals more fully with your relationship with your children and the legacy you are living and leaving for them. How would you like to be remembered by your children? What two or three phrases would you most want them to use in describing you as a man and as a father?

## LESSON NINE
# LIVING A LEGACY FOR YOUR CHILDREN

### LOCATION

1. Thinking back over memorable sporting events, what moment comes to mind that spelled disaster: a mental mistake that cost a game, a failed hand-off that lost a race, a dropped pass that spelled defeat, and so forth?

2. What's the difference between "leaving a legacy" and "living a legacy"?

3. What are some of your most valued items of the legacy you've been given by those who have been most influential for you?

### CLUES

*Key Scriptures:* Joshua 24:15; Psalm 78:5-7; Matthew 6:19-21; Mark 4:19; Romans 8:37; 1 Corinthians 9:24-27; Ephesians 6:4; Philippians 1:23; 3:13-14; 2 Timothy 1:4-5; Hebrews 11:13; 12:1-2; 1 Peter 2:11

4. What are the three key components of a spiritual legacy (pp. 155, 160, 164)?

    1.

    2.

    3.

5. What does it mean for a father to live "in view of eternity"?

6. Do you agree that too often we "worship our work, work at our play, and play at our worship" (p. 164)? How can we counteract this imbalance?

### DIRECTION

7. What "baggage" do you need to lose in order to "run a strong race" (see p. 161)?

8. What is one decision that you made at least five years ago about which you continue to be glad today?

9. What decisions have you made recently, or what decisions are you now considering, with the understanding that, even though they may present hardship now, you know you will not regret them in the future?

# PART FOUR SESSION
# A MAN OF GOD AND
# HIS MINISTRY

## LOCATION

1. What do you think is more challenging for a man: to have a mentor, or to be a mentor? Why?

2. What connects you with a local church? How strong is that connection?

3. Think of a time recently when you shared or showed your faith. What happened?

## CLUES

4. We looked at parallel reasons for *having* a mentor and *being* a mentor. Which of those reasons do you find most compelling? Why?

5. How did the chapter *Sharing Our Lord, Our Light, and Our Labor* sharpen your view of the church? What changes did you feel challenged to make?

6. What obstacles do you find toughest to overcome in responding to Jesus' command to spread the gospel? What encouragement did you find in chapter 12?

## DIRECTION

7. What difference do you think this book would have made in your life if you had read it twenty years ago? Why?

8. What three decisions or changes are you in the process of making as a result of reading this book? Write them on a card to carry in your wallet and refer to from time to time.

    1.

    2.

    3.

9. Read the "4 Sakes Prayer" noted below and then spend some time praying with your group about what you know it will take for you and them to see this prayer come true for all of you.

**4 Sakes Prayer**
*For the sake of the Kingdom,*
*For the sake of my family,*
*For the sake of God's church,*
*And for the sake of our nation,*
*I will become a man of God.*

## Lesson Ten

# The Need to Have and to Be a Mentor

## Location

1. This chapter begins with a description of coach John Wooden as a mentor to his players. What is the role of a mentor?

2. Who was your best mentor? What made him so effective and helpful?

3. Describe a unique learning experience you had with a mentor.

## Clues

*Key Scriptures:* 2 Samuel 11–12; Acts 4:36-37; 11:23-26; 1 Corinthians 9:24, 27; 15:58; 2 Corinthians 6:17; Philippians 2:4; 4:13; 2 Timothy 1:14; 2:1-7; James 1:8; 2 Peter 1:3; Jude 3

4. What three reasons are given to back up the assertion that every man needs to *have* a mentor (pp. 171-173)?

5. What three reasons are given to back up the assertion that every man needs to *be* a mentor (pp. 173-177)? In what ways do the answers for questions 4 and 5 compare? Why?

6. Identify at least one Bible example for each of the four essential qualities of a mentor (pp. 177-182).

7. What's your reaction to the chain of connections between Edward Kimball and Billy Graham?

## Direction

8. As you think about mentoring, identify five people who presently mentor or could have a mentoring role in your life. Then list five others for whom you might serve as a mentor.

Mentors:

1.

2.

3.

4.

5.

People Whom I Could Mentor:

1.

2.

3.

4.

5.

9. Of the names in the first list above, whom would you be willing to approach this week with a specific request for further mentoring? Of the names on the second list, to whom could you offer this week to be a more intentional mentor? What would you say to him?

LESSON ELEVEN

# SHARING OUR LORD, OUR LIGHT, AND OUR LABOR

## LOCATION

1. Describe one of your most unforgettable moments of connection with other Christians in God's presence.

2. African-American pastor and teacher Tony Evans enjoys telling racially mixed audiences of American Christians, "We may have come over here on different ships, but we're in the same boat now" (p. 186). What does he mean?

3. Suppose that someone who claims not to be a Christian were to ask you, "What do you people mean when you talk about fellowship?" How would you answer?

## CLUES

*Key Scriptures:* Genesis 32:24-32; Isaiah 40:31; Matthew 25:21; Mark 10:45; 14:6-8; Luke 10:38-42; John 8:12; Romans 12:1; 1 Corinthians 4:2; 12:4, 11; 2 Corinthians 12:9-10; Philippians 4:13; Hebrews 2:11; 11; 1 John 1:1-7; Revelation 3:20

4. How is the word *koinonia* explained (p. 186)? What three big characteristics do believers in Jesus have in common?

5. Use the points described here (pp. 186-188) to develop an explanation of what you mean when you say, "Jesus is Lord."

6. In what ways is shared faith a shared light (pp. 188-189)?

7. What insights do you draw from Alan Redpath's comments on the preacher's statement, "You can have a saved soul, but a lost life" (p. 190)?

## DIRECTION

8. What further steps do you need to take in order to identify your spiritual gifts or place them into service?

9. On pages 194-197, we read about various qualities that can be found in genuine service. To which one of these do you need to pay the most attention? Why?

## LESSON TWELVE
# A COMMISSION TO MARKETPLACE EVANGELISM

### LOCATION

1. Describe at least three environments that make up what you would call your personal marketplace in life.

2. Outside of "religious situations," what clues would someone have that you are a follower of Jesus?

3. What word most closely expresses your initial attitude toward most people you meet? (For example: lost, good, friendly, customer, sinner, needy, etc.)

### CLUES

*Key Scriptures:* Ecclesiastes 3:11; Isaiah 40:8; Matthew 5:16; 10:16; 28:19-20; John 9; Acts 1:8; 26; Romans 1:16; 3:23; 6:23; 9:2-4; 1 Corinthians 15:1-4; 2 Corinthians 3:4-5; 5:20; Ephesians 1:3; 4:1; 5:2, 15-18; 6:12-18; 2 Timothy 4:5; Hebrews 2:15; 9:27; 1 Peter 3:15

4. In your own words, express the four needs every person has that only Jesus can meet (pp. 201-203):

    1.

    2.

    3.

    4.

5. In what ways can you share with others the four gifts Jack says believers can give someone who is lost (pp. 203-209)? (Describe them in terms of your life.)

    1.

    2.

    3.

    4.

6. What would you say in response to this statement on page 210: "In fact, I believe that if anything, the church of Jesus Christ has been guilty of *under-challenging* men to step up and take spiritual leadership"? Include examples with your answer.

## DIRECTION

7. Turn each of the last challenges in the book into a description of a personal action plan for steps toward becoming a man of God:

A. I will act on the *time to look up* by . . .

B. I will act on the *time to step up* by . . .

C. I will act on the *time to wise up* by . . .

D. I will act on the *time to gear* up by . . .

8. In this study's introductory session, we suggested a prayer based on Jack's approach to the very personal issue of becoming a man of God. Read this prayer again and then note how your understanding of its significance has changed since you began this study.

**4 Sakes Prayer**
*For the sake of the Kingdom,*
*For the sake of my family,*
*For the sake of God's church,*
*And for the sake of our nation,*
*I will become a man of God.*

9. Describe at least one "life-objective" that has shifted for you during this study.